Collins

LITTLE BOOKS

GIN

HarperCollins Publishers
Westerhill Road
Bishopbriggs
Glasgow
G64 2QT

First Edition 2017

Reprint 10 9 8 7 6 5 4 3 2 1 0

© HarperCollins Publishers 2017

ISBN 978-0-00-825810-8

Collins® is a registered trademark
of HarperCollins Publishers Limited

www.collins.co.uk

A catalogue record for this book is
available from the British Library

Author: Dominic Roskrow

Typeset by
Davidson Publishing Solutions

Printed and bound in
China by RR Donnelley APS Co Ltd

Contents

Introduction   5

What is gin and how is it made?   9

A – Z of gins   16

Index   216

About the Author

Dominic Roskrow is an award-winning drinks writer and magazine editor. He specializes in whisky and has written twelve books on the subject. He has edited *The Spirits Business*, *Club Mirror*, *Pub Business*, and *Whisky Magazine*, writes a spirits column for *Drinks International*, and has contributed to dozens of newspapers and magazines across the world. He was Fortnum & Mason Drinks Writer of the Year in 2015. His most recent book, *Whisky: Japan*, was chosen as Britain's best spirits book in the Gourmand Food and Drink Awards and is shortlisted for the title of Gourmand World's Best Spirit Book.

Dominic is one of only a few people to be chosen as a Keeper of the Quaich for his work on Scotch whisky, and to be appointed a Kentucky Colonel for his promotion of bourbon. Dominic is an avid Leicester City and All Blacks fan, and loves loud heavy rock music.

Introduction

In one form or other gin has been with us for more than 600 years. It has been subject to wild swings of fortune, to gigantic ebbs and flows in popularity, and been courted and rejected by prince and pauper alike. In its many guises it has served as a medicine to the affluent, a tonic to the troops, and an elixir to the wretched rabble that populated the violent streets of London. Today it is enjoying a worldwide revival and has achieved a status as the very epitome of quality craft distilling.

Gin's roots lie in Europe, quite possibly in Italy but most definitely in the Netherlands, where it was distilled for medicine, and juniper was first used to hide the taste of the naked spirit. It was given to British troops fighting in the Thirty Years War – Dutch courage – and it may be that returning troops brought it back, increasing its popularity, though a limited amount of distillation had already started in England by this time.

The better made 'Dutch' version of the spirit was enjoyed by the aristocracy, and a poorer, cheaper spirit became popular with the poor. When Dutch King William of Orange ascended the throne, he encouraged distillation and there may have been some patriotic consumption too. By 1730 there were more than 7000 shops in London selling nothing but spirits.

But gin had started to become a problem. Attempts to restrict widespread drunkenness and violence by making gin prohibitively expensive backfired spectacularly, prompting rioting and a surge in illicit distilling. Few official licences were taken out, but production in London reached a staggering 11,000,000 gallons.

By this time further licensing reforms meant that beer shops had sprung up across the country. To compete, gin distillers opened large gin palaces – imposing and relatively stylish places. But gin was about to undergo another sea change. The invention of the column still meant that the quality of gin in general rose, and a specific style of gin came into existence: London Dry Gin.

Gin became popular with the middle classes, and when the Empire spread out to India, its transformation was completed when it was discovered that quinine was a deterrent to malaria-carrying mosquitoes – and the perfect way to hide its bitter taste was to mix it with carbonated water and add it to gin, creating the gin and tonic.

By the twentieth century, though, it seemed gin's best days were behind it. The spirit faced a two-pronged identity crisis. On the one hand, its debauched and negative reputation proved remarkably enduring – 'gin-soaked' and 'mother's ruin' are not extinct even now. And on the other, the gin and tonic gained a reputation associated with the worse type of Englishman – and it did tend to be men – those associated with the closed-shop world of the golf club and sports bar, and the pre-drinks ritual when dining out.

Gin's fortunes were revived in the 1970s, when cocktails became popular and drinks makers discovered recipes where gin was a key ingredient. Perhaps, then, we shouldn't have been surprised by the surge in popularity in gin when a new generation of bartenders – now calling themselves mixologists – turned to provenance and history to create creative and exciting new cocktails. Nonetheless, today's gin boom is unprecedented. A perfect wave of a thriving cocktail culture, a desire to drink less but better, a trend towards heritage and authenticity, and a worldwide passion for micro and craft distilling has meant the emergence of hundreds of new gins.

No book could hope to cover them all, nor reflect the surge of renewed interest in flavoured gins, aged gins, innovative new drinks based loosely on gin, and close relatives such as genevers, and this book doesn't even attempt to do so. To put it into some context, one major online retailer lists nearly 450 gins. That's just the tip of the iceberg. The number of new producers is growing by the week. It seems that every town, city, and even village is producing its own gin, and not just in England, either. Indeed, most British gin is produced in Scotland.

The loose definitions of what constitutes gin means that long-standing controversies as to the importance of juniper to a gin's taste and the way it is distilled continue unabated. Some of the experimentation and innovation in the category mean that, effectively, new drinks categories are being invented.

But, whatever else, the craft revolution means that gin has shaken off its snooty middle-class English image, and is enjoying a surge of popularity among drinkers seeking quality and well-made drinks.

This book is meant to be an introduction to the gin category. We have selected one hundred gins, covering the best-known names and a selection of the best of the new wave of gin makers. We have concentrated mainly on traditional gins.

So what exactly is gin?

What is gin and how is it made?

Unlike the production of Scottish single malt whisky, which is covered by a stringent set of rules, there is considerable debate as to what may be acceptably called gin.

The basic definition of gin is a spirit made from ethyl alcohol and flavoured with botanicals. Juniper berries must be included and should be the 'predominant' flavour. The alcoholic strength of the spirit must be no less than 37.5% ABV. There are further definitions as to what can be called distilled gin and London gin.

But the definitions are loose and leave considerable loopholes and room for interpretation. There have been attempts to tighten up the rules, but some distillers have played footloose and fancy-free with the requirement to have a 'predominant' juniper flavour.

Making gin
In simplistic terms, gin is made from a base spirit that has been distilled to a high strength and then reduced to 60% ABV. Some distilleries make this base spirit themselves, but many buy it in from a select number of large distilleries.

The spirit, made from a variety of grains, is sometimes referred to as neutral grain spirit, though that is not quite the case, and the spirit used will influence the final gin. To this base spirit a range of botanicals will be added. These are natural ingredients and include the compulsory juniper berries, as well as, most often used, coriander, angelica, lemon, and orange peel.

The number of botanicals varies from gin to gin, but a good-quality premium gin may have six to ten botanicals, and these may include everything from spices to tea and from flowers to exotic fruits.

Steeping
Some distillers soak the botanicals before distillation, and they have their own ideas how long this process should take.

Immersion
The botanicals are then immersed in the base spirit, normally in a pot still. The pot still is then heated to release the oils from the botanicals. At this point the process is similar to that for single malt whisky production, with the early vapours discarded, the middle part of the run collected, and the final part discarded. Further neutral alcohol and water may be added.

Vapour extraction
Some distilleries do not immerse the botanicals, but suspend them above the base spirit. This is the method used by Bombay Sapphire. As the vapours rise, the flavours of the suspended botanicals are extracted and collected as before.

Individual extraction and blending
Some distillers take each botanical separately and put it through the distillation process. Then the collection of different botanical distillates are blended to produce the required gin.

What this book covers

It is hard to believe that in the early part of the millennium gin was restricted to Gordon's, Beefeater, and a smattering of premium expressions. Now a good bar will offer the customer an array of regionally produced premium gins in a range of styles and flavours, quite possibly alongside a choice of mixers. No longer is the lemon slice the lone accompaniment to the classic gin and tonic.

Tonics matter, as does the ice used. And discerning drinkers now understand what makes a good martini or negroni, as well as a gin and tonic.

And that is the tip of the iceberg. The new generation of mixologists are working at the coal face by exploring old drinks styles and historical recipes, looking to experiment with botanicals, and rediscovering and re-inventing classic old drinks such as The Old Tom.

Apart from a passing reference to these drinks styles, this book is firmly focused on what might be described as the more traditional gin brands. Our selection includes a mixture of the major producers, alongside some of the more exciting of the new producers and one or two which show just how vibrant and exciting the gin sector has become.

Gin-related spirits: genever

Genever is often referred to as 'Dutch gin' but this is not quite right. Under European law it may be made in the Netherlands, in Belgium, and in a couple of German and French states. Though it is related to gin and is seen to be the forerunner of the premium gin spirit now being made in Britain, it also nods towards the production of whiskey, and particularly bourbon.

Genever is made from a mash bill made up of rye, corn, and malted barley. The grains are cooked at different temperatures, milled and mashed by adding hot water. This is then fermented into a rough beer or barley wine. The yeast used is normally baker's yeast, but brewer's or distiller's yeast may also be used.

The resulting liquid is then distilled up to three times. Finally the resulting distillate is distilled again with a range of botanicals which must include juniper berries. The resulting genever is fruity and infused with botanicals.

Oude or jonge

Genever may, and often is, matured in barrels at this point. And it may be described as either 'oude' or 'jonge'. Somewhat confusingly, this does not refer to the length of time the spirit spends in wood. A jonge genever contains a maximum of 15 per cent malt, and often a lot less. Oude genevers must have a minimum of 15 per cent malt wine content, and typically have 40 per cent, giving them more character.

Genevers are most often matured for a short period in used casks, but some are aged for considerably longer, and the likes of Zuidam in the Netherlands is using a range of cask types.

Gin-related spirits: Old Tom

Nobody is absolutely sure where the name Old Tom comes from, but you'd be forgiven if you thought it had something to do with the expression 'any old Tom, Dick, or Harry', because it would seem it can be many things to many people.

Just as its naming is lost in the depths of time, so it would seem is an exact definition of it, but, in simplistic terms, it is a maltier, fruitier, and sweeter version of what we might now associate with traditional gin.

It occupies a space between the big, rich, malty genevers that the Dutch produced, and the sharper, tangy, and drier style of gin that we know as London Dry Gin. Walk into a gin palace or pub in the 18th or 19th century and order a gin, and Old Tom is likely to be what you would get. But by the 20th century its popularity had declined and London-style gin had replaced it.

The picture is further clouded by the fact that distillation techniques were evolving rapidly, there were no uniform or standardized methods of production, and, beyond the need for juniper berries to be among the botanicals, ingredients for it weren't set in stone. Some Old Tom was exported in tired old barrels that didn't influence the flavour of the spirit, while others travelled in active barrels and matured en route, giving them very different flavours.

The Old Tom style is being rediscovered, and leading drinks experts such as Dave Wondrich have worked with distillers to produce a modern version of the drink. Many consider the style to be the perfect stepping stone for a whisky lover to discover the joys of gin.

Gin-related spirits: Aged gins

The whisky writer Jim Murray tells a story about being with a Dutch distiller describing his latest gin, which he had aged in oak barrels for some years. As the conversation went on and they talked more about the grain used and the type of barrel, Jim suddenly declared, 'That's not gin, that's whisky!'

It's a fine line, but certainly once you remove the botanicals from the equation, the lines become severely blurred. Aged gin has become fashionable in recent years, with bars hosting their own mini-casks full of gin spirit, and creating their own take on aged gin.

There are also countries, particularly those in Eastern Europe, where stainless steel casks are prohibitively expensive and distillers have had no choice but to use oak casks.

Given the flexibility that gin offers, the idea of ageing opens up a whole new world of possible flavours, as distillers explore everything from virgin oak from continents across the world to casks that have been previously used for a vast range of different wines and spirits, including some that are highly regional and region-specific.

Gin-related spirits: Flavoured gins

This is where modern gin gets most exciting, or where the category is being devalued or destroyed, depending on your point of view. Purists say that flavoured gins are not gins at all, but are flavoured vodkas, particularly where juniper is relegated to the passenger seat. Others argue that there is no difference between these gins and liqueurs.

But it's not that simple. Firstly, the flavours aren't added in the most direct sense, but are infused with the gin spirit during distillation, or as part of a maturation process in the cask. And while the natural reaction is to assume that some of the concoctions sound sickly, cloying, and oversweet, that doesn't need to be the case at all. A new wave of gin distillers argue that they are inventing new styles and exciting new drinks, whether they are strictly gin or not.

Sources for flavoured gins that have been used in the past include Shiraz grapes, clotted cream, quince, and Yorkshire tea. But a special mention needs to go to Sikkim, a Spanish gin using red tea from Sikkim, Tibet, mixed with, among other things, wild strawberries, cranberries, bilberries, bitter orange, and coriander. It is described as pleasant, tasty, and refreshing.

6 O'clock

PRODUCER: Bramley & Gage

ABV: 43%

REGION AND COUNTRY OF ORIGIN: Gloucestershire, England

WEBSITE: www.bramleyandgage.com/6-oclock

BOTANICALS: Includes juniper berries, orange peel, elderflower

Bramley & Gage is a company originally founded by husband-and-wife team Edward Bramley Kane and Penelope Gage, who were fruit farmers in Devon. They started making fruit liqueurs in the 1980s and became rather good at it, expanding the drinks side of the business. The company is now run by a new generation of Kanes. This expression of gin was launched in 2010, and is named after the time when the great-grandfather of current directors Michael and Felicity would sit down for a gin and tonic. This stylishly packaged gin is distilled on a two-hundred-litre still known as Kathleen, and it is one of a range of products that include a sloe gin and a damson gin. The company has expanded over the last thirty years, and is now based in Gloucestershire. 6 O'clock has won countless awards, and can be tasted as part of the distillery's tour and tasting package.

60 Squared

PRODUCER: Anno Distillers

ABV: 60%

REGION AND COUNTRY OF ORIGIN: Kent, England

WEBSITE: www.annodistillers.co.uk

BOTANICALS: Juniper, orris root, coriander, angelica, cassia bark, liquorice, cubebs, Kentish hops, Kentish lavender, Kentish rosehips, camomile, Kentish samphire, lemon, bitter orange, kaffir lime leaves

This is another gin from Anno Distillers, which makes Kent Dry Gin, and uses local botanicals including Kentish hops and lavender in its recipes.

This gin was originally released as a limited edition of 1,000 bottles to celebrate founders Andy Reason and Norman Lewis's sixtieth birthdays. However, the distillery says that because of the overwhelmingly positive response it received from consumers, the distillery has decided to continue with it. As it was a celebratory release, the distillers say they made sure that the flavour would burst in the mouth. This was done by combining a selection of local hops, woody botanicals, and enticing spices with a full 60% ABV. The bold flavours work particularly well in a negroni. Just months after its release, Anno 60 Squared claimed the title of 'Specialist Drinks Category Winner' at the Taste of Kent Awards in March 2016.

Adnams Copper House

PRODUCER: Adnams

ABV: 40%

REGION AND COUNTRY OF ORIGIN: Southwold, England

WEBSITE: www.adnams.co.uk/spirits/our-spirits/distilled-gin

BOTANICALS: Juniper berries, orris root, coriander seed, cardamom pod, sweet orange peel, hibiscus flowers

Adnams is a highly respected award-winning brewer, but it had always been a desire of chairman Jonathan Adnam to make distilled products including whisky. Copper House was built on the brewery's Southwold site after the company successfully overturned arcane rules that forbade brewing and distillation under the same roof. Distiller John McCarthy and his team now make a range of distilled products, but this was the starting point, and it has won awards regularly. The distillery points to the use of hibiscus flowers as the least expected ingredient. The team say they fell in love with the hibiscus petals' bitter floral taste when they tasted it in hibiscus tea. The distillery also makes an enjoyable eau de vie based on its Broadside bitter.

Anno Kent Dry Gin

PRODUCER: Anno Distillers

ABV: 43%

REGION AND COUNTRY OF ORIGIN: Marden, Kent, England

WEBSITE: www.annodistillers.co.uk

BOTANICALS: Juniper, orris root, coriander, angelica, cassia bark, liquorice, cubebs, Kentish hops, Kentish lavender, Kentish rosehips, camomile, Kentish samphire, lemon, bitter orange, kaffir lime leaves

The co-founders of Anno Distillers are bringing a scientific approach to the making of a gin, but they have combined the classroom ethos with a friendship and trust borne of years working together, and combined it with a joint passion for great-tasting spirits.

Research and development chemists Andy Reason and Norman Lewis took early retirement from GlaxoSmithKline in 2011 and set about creating premium gin. With the help of Andy's daughter Kim, who handles the marketing side of the business, they have created a gin that stays close to
a traditional gin model but gives it a Kent twist with a range of locally produced botanicals. The gin is produced

Aviation American Gin

PRODUCER: Davos Brands

ABV: 42%

REGION AND COUNTRY OF ORIGIN: Portland, USA

WEBSITE: www.aviationgin.com

BOTANICALS: Juniper berries, *Eletaria cardamomum*, lavender, sarsaparilla, coriander, anise seed, dried sweet orange peel

Aviation Gin is the result of a special partnership between Portland's House Spirits Distillery and bartender Ryan Magarian, who shared a vision of creating a renegade regional gin brand. The aim was to move away from an overdependence on juniper and to push forward the rich floral and savoury notes of the spices and flowers common in the Pacific Northwest. This, the team argued, would create a decidedly American style of gin. The name Aviation is inspired by a cocktail created at New York's Hotel Wallick, containing gin, maraschino liqueur, and freshly squeezed lemon juice. It gave Ryan Magarian the inspiration to create exciting cocktails with gin.

Barr Hill Gin

PRODUCER: Caledonia Spirits

ABV: 42%

REGION AND COUNTRY OF ORIGIN: Vermont, USA

WEBSITE: www.caledoniaspirits.com

BOTANICALS: Juniper berries, honey

There's a bee in the logo of Caledonia Spirits, producer of Barr Hill Gin and its sister, Tom Cat, which is aged in new oak barrels. And honey is key to the spirits, produced in Caledonia County, Vermont. This gin uses raw honey provided by the region's bees, and the name refers to the inspiration behind this gin, the view from the top of Barr Hill Nature Reserve. The inspiration for the distillery comes from Todd Hardie, who first bought a beehive aged twelve, and who ran Honey Gardens Apiaries for thirty years, before teaming up with local home-brew store owner Ryan Christiansen, who is now head distiller at Caledonia. The company has been making gin and vodka since 2009 and has struggled to keep up with exceptional demand.

Beefeater 24

PRODUCER: Pernod Ricard

ABV: 45%

REGION AND COUNTRY OF ORIGIN: London, England

WEBSITE: www.beefeatergin.com

BOTANICALS: Juniper berries, Japanese sencha tea, Chinese green tea, grapefruit peel, lemon peel, almonds, Seville orange peel, coriander seed, orris root, liquorice root, angelica root, angelica seed

Beefeater is, of course, one of the great gin brands, but this brings an Eastern twist to the basic recipe, and includes both Japanese and Chinese tea in the ingredients. The idea came about when master distiller Desmond Payne was travelling in Japan and decided to mix some Beefeater with green tea. You'd have to ask him why, but the resulting drink – giving a whole new meaning to the name G & T – inspired him to spend the next eighteen months experimenting with different teas and botanicals before settling on this. Beefeater 24 is described as a smooth and citrus-flavoured gin ideal for making modern cocktails.

Berkeley Square

PRODUCER: Greenall's

ABV: 40%

REGION AND COUNTRY OF ORIGIN: Warrington, England

WEBSITE: www.berkeleysquaregin.com

BOTANICALS: Juniper, angelica, coriander seeds, cubeb berries, lavender, sage, basil, kaffir lime leaves

Greenall's is traditionally a highly respected brewer from the northwest of England, but the company took over the fine distillery in Warrington some years back. It now produces its own range of gins including this one, as well as distilling for others. This gin associates itself with the style and glamour of London's Mayfair and lays claim to being based on 700 years of tradition. It also draws a parallel between the finely crafted product here and the finest single malts. This is a delicate gin, made using pure water from a source that runs from the Welsh borders to the edge of the Pennines. The lavender, sage, and basil are grown locally, and their aromas are extracted through steeping and then gentle distillation.

Black Shuck

PRODUCER: Norfolk Sloe Company

ABV: 43%

REGION AND COUNTRY OF ORIGIN: Norfolk, England

WEBSITE: thenorfolksloecompany.com

BOTANICALS: Juniper berries, coriander, bitter orange peel with Norfolk lavender and Norfolk sea buckthorn.

You may recognize the name of this gin from the song by Suffolk hard rock band The Darkness. It refers to a legendary black dog with flaming red eyes that is said to have roamed the land and coast of Suffolk and Norfolk for centuries. Some believe that the dog's legend stems from Norse mythology, others to a boating accident that claimed the lives of a Saxon and a Danish fisherman. This gin, says the distillery, is the antidote if the Black Shuck is sighted and brings you misfortune. The gin is made with local Norfolk botanicals, and is stylish and impressive, having a distinctive, aromatic taste with some irresistible floral notes.

Blackwater No.5 Gin

PRODUCER: Blackwater

ABV: 41.5%

REGION AND COUNTRY OF ORIGIN: Waterford, Ireland

WEBSITE: www.blackwaterdistillery.ie

BOTANICALS: Juniper, bitter orange, lemon, lemongrass, coriander, liquorice root, angelica root, cinnamon, quills, myrtle pepper, bitter almond, green cardamom, orris root

Ireland's first craft gin distillery sits on the banks of the Blackwater River in west Waterford, a county once known for being the largest importer of spice in the country. Today the distillery wishes to keep the essence of Waterford's colourful history while maintaining the quality and skill to perfect the best gin they can. The man behind this distillery is spirits writer and television producer Peter Mulryan. He's a no-nonsense sort of guy who doesn't like gimmicks, so the distillery is deliberately old-school, and everything is done by hand. Pushing and pulling the many levers, taps, handles, and dials takes the distillers longer but they believe that this way they can truly capture their unique style in a bottle.

Blackwoods Vintage Dry Gin

PRODUCER: Blackwoods Distillers

ABV: 60%

REGION AND COUNTRY OF ORIGIN: Shetland, Scotland

WEBSITE: www.blackwoodsgin.co.uk

BOTANICALS: Juniper berries, angelica, coriander, citrus peel, cinnamon, liquorice, nutmeg, sea pink, marsh marigold, meadowsweet

The Shetland Isles, off Scotland's rugged northern coastline, are sited on the sixty-degrees line of latitude, and that is the inspiration for this weighty gin. It is released in limited editions, and each batch varies depending on what botanicals are available on the islands. Blackwoods is specifically Shetland because of the presence of botanicals such as the rugged sea pink, a pink flower which grows on the coastline in a limited window of late May to early July; marsh marigold, which is a yellow flower and a larger version of the buttercup, and which grows from April to June; and the sweet-scented and honeyish meadowsweet. This version is aimed at the serious mixologist making complex cocktails, but there is a more standard 40% version also available.

Bloom

PRODUCER: Greenall's

ABV: 40%

REGION AND COUNTRY OF ORIGIN: Warrington, England

WEBSITE: www.bloomgin.com

BOTANICALS: Juniper berries, coriander, angelica, cubeb berries, honeysuckle, camomile, pomelo

This sophisticated, subtle, floral gin is the creation of the highly respected gin master distiller Joanne Moore, who has worked at G&J Distillery in Warrington since 1996 and has been a master distiller there for more than ten years. This has been deliberately created to reflect her love of nature. It's something of a global concoction, with botanicals including honeysuckle and pomelo from China, juniper berries from Tuscany, and camomile from France. That said, Moore has retained some key aromas of an English country garden, and the juniper notes are muted to allow delicate floral aromas to take centre stage. It is suggested you enjoy Bloom with strawberries – ideal in the summer.

Boë

PRODUCER: VC2 Brands

ABV: 41.5%

REGION AND COUNTRY OF ORIGIN: Stirling, Scotland

WEBSITE: www.boegin.com

BOTANICALS: Juniper berries, coriander, cardamom, angelica, ginger, almonds, orris root, cassia bark, liquorice, orange, lemon, cubeb berry

'In the year 1658 world renowned Professor Franz de la Boë gently infused a clear grain spirit with hand picked juniper berries while painstakingly searching for a medicinal tonic. Franz de la Boë invented the world's first GIN!'

Big words, but you'll find them on the website of Boë Gin, which is made at the Deanston Distillery near Stirling in Scotland. And the whisky distillery's master distiller was convinced enough to take the name for this lovingly created and stylishly packaged gin. In addition to the main bottling, which is made in small batches, the distillery makes a violet-infused gin, and a peach and hibiscus flavoured gin liqueur.

Bombay Dry Gin

PRODUCER: Bacardi

ABV: 40%

REGION AND COUNTRY OF ORIGIN: Laverstock, Hampshire, England

WEBSITE: www.bacardilimited.com

BOTANICALS: Juniper berries, coriander, orris root, lemon peel, angelica root, almond, liquorice root, cassia bark

Before there was Bombay Sapphire there was Bombay Dry Gin, and this isn't as flash as its sibling. Indeed, it's a solid, no-fuss central defender of a gin, and it's as good a representation of a London Dry Gin as you're going to find. It is a re-creation and tweaking of a traditional recipe that stretches back to the 18th century. A quick look at the botanicals used will reveal that it's a straight-shooter, with all the traditional elements in place, and it's none the worse for that. The 'Bombay' part of the name stretches back to the 1960s, and it is said to reflect gin's popularity in India.

Bombay Sapphire

PRODUCER: Bacardi

ABV: 40%

REGION AND COUNTRY OF ORIGIN: Laverstock, Hampshire, England

WEBSITE: www.bacardilimited.com/our-brands/bombay-sapphire/

BOTANICALS: Juniper berries, coriander, orris root, lemon peel, angelica root, almond, liquorice root, cassia bark, cubeb berries, grains of paradise

There's a metaphorical swagger about Bombay Sapphire. It's a brand that knows its significance and it's happy to flaunt it. While big brother Bombay Dry lurks at the back of the web, Bombay Sapphire has a bright and all-singing website with distillery details, complete with tour booking form. Bombay Sapphire was the launchpad for the current gin revolution, by offering a quality gin with a lighter, easier taste. It has two additional botanicals, and it is carefully distilled at Laverstock Distillery. Confident marketing, a different gin taste, and the distinctive blue bottle restoked gin's fires and arguably opened the door for the plethora of new and less juniper-intense gins that have followed.

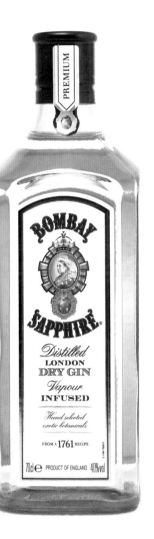

Broker's Gin

PRODUCER: Martin and Andy Dawson

ABV: 47%

REGION AND COUNTRY OF ORIGIN: West Midlands, England

WEBSITE: www.brokersgin.com

BOTANICALS: Juniper berries, angelica root, cassia bark, cinnamon, coriander, lemon peel, liquorice root, nutmeg, orange peel, orris root

The top of the bottle has a bowler hat on it, reflecting the fact that the producers consider gin a quintessentially English drink. The name refers to the very English stockbroker image, and the website is a little starched and staid, but it would seem that tongue is very firmly in cheek when it comes to Broker's. Not that there's anything comical about this much-awarded and somewhat traditional gin, which its makers say is made to an old recipe in a two-hundred-year-old distillery in the heart of England. The base spirit is made from wheat, and is quadruple-distilled and then redistilled with ten traditional botanicals on a traditional pot still. A seriously good gin with a quirky marketing approach, say the owners. Fair enough.

Cadenhead's Classic

PRODUCER: Hayman's for Cadenhead

ABV: 50%

REGION AND COUNTRY OF ORIGIN: Witham, England

WEBSITE: www.wmcadenhead.com

BOTANICALS: Juniper berries, coriander, Seville orange peel, lemon peel, liquorice, angelica root, orris, cinnamon, cassia quills, nutmeg

William Cadenhead is the independent bottling arm of J & A Mitchell, owners of Springbank whisky distillery in Campbeltown, in the west of Scotland. It buys its gin from the highly respected gin producer Hayman's, and has been bottling gin since 1972. It produces three different gins of three different strengths and all to the same basic recipe, though this one doesn't include saffron as the other two do. The gins are diluted at Cadenhead's headquarters and bottled. This has the highest strength of the three and the alcoholic bite reinforces the juniper and angelica flavours. This gin has a solid international reputation and will appeal to fans of traditional gin.

Cambridge Dry Gin

PRODUCER: Will and Lucy Lowe

ABV: 42%

REGION AND COUNTRY OF ORIGIN: Cambridge, England

WEBSITE: www.cambridgedistillery.co.uk

BOTANICALS: Juniper berries, blackcurrant leaf, basil, rosemary, lemon verbena, rose petals, violet petals, angelica seed

If you want to know the meaning of the word 'bespoke', look no further than the Cambridge Distillery – or at least the person behind it. Will Lowe has tailored gin recipes to meet individual tastes, built up a business creating gins specifically for high-end restaurants, and now makes small-batch gins, aided by his wife Lucy. Among his creations are a Japanese gin, and Anty Gin, each bottle of which contains the essence of more than sixty red wood ants. This has been produced to capitalize on Lowe's two seasonal gins, which sell out within days of launch. Each botanical is distilled individually in volumes of less than two litres before being blended into the final gin.

Caorunn

PRODUCER: Balmenach

ABV: 41.8%

REGION AND COUNTRY OF ORIGIN: Cromdale, Scotland

WEBSITE: www.caorunngin.com

BOTANICALS: Juniper berries, coriander seed, orange peel, lemon peel, angelica root, cassia bark, rowan berries, bog myrtle, heather, Coul blush apples, dandelion leaf

Caorunn is another Scottish gin with a huge whisky link. It is made at Balmenach Distillery, a whisky distillery that makes a powerful and weighty single malt. This is very different – a gentle, floral, and delicate fine gin made with eleven botanicals: the big six classic gin ones, and five collected in the Highlands to reflect the drink's strong Scottish heritage. The Speyside region is widely acclaimed as a distilling region without peer, for the high water quality, the regional flavours, and the skill of gin master Simon Bailey. This is a special gin made in 1,000-litre batches by vaporizing the spirit through what the distillery claims is the world's only working copper berry chamber – a horizontal chamber containing trays on which the botanicals are placed and over which the vaporized spirits pass.

CAORUNN
{ka-roon}

70cl℮   SMALL BATCH SCOTTISH GIN   41.8% vol.
Balmenach Distillery Stéidhichte 1824

Citadelle

PRODUCER: Cognac Ferrand

ABV: 44%

REGION AND COUNTRY OF ORIGIN: Southwest France

WEBSITE: www.citadellegin.com

BOTANICALS: Not fully disclosed, but nineteen botanicals, including juniper berries, cinnamon, nutmeg, génépi

The producers of Citadelle, a French gin produced in the southwest of the country, using botanicals from the Italian and French Alps, have unearthed a history that reveals that in the 18th century, when France and England were almost permanently at war, the French authorities encouraged English smugglers to collect French genever in a bid to undermine the British economy. Not only that, but there was, apparently, great demand for French genever in England. Certainly, Citadelle is stylish and different. Patience is all here: the botanicals are immersed for seventy-two hours before being distilled for twelve hours in small pot stills over a naked flame.

City of London Gin

PRODUCER: City of London Distillery

ABV: 40%

REGION AND COUNTRY OF ORIGIN: London, England

WEBSITE: www.cityoflondondistillery.com

BOTANICALS: Juniper berries, angelica root, liquorice, grapefruit peel, lemon peel, orange peel, coriander

The story of gin in London is an amazing and dramatic one. There was a time when there was a gin palace or a shop selling gin in every street, and yet for a period of almost two hundred years there weren't any distilleries at all. When gin came back to the city, it did so through two distilleries with virtually the same name. This is one of them, and it has been making gin in London since 2012. This is a traditional London Dry Gin. City of London also makes premium gins under the names Christopher Wren and Square Mile. The distillery is in the heart of London and has a public bar so you can try before you buy.

SCENE IN A LONDON GIN "PALACE."

Cold River

PRODUCER: Cold River

ABV: 47%

REGION AND COUNTRY OF ORIGIN: Freeport, USA

WEBSITE: www.coldrivervodka.com/gin

BOTANICALS: Seven undisclosed botanicals but including juniper berries, and blueberries

Cold River is an American craft spirits producer in Maine, and it prides itself on making small-batch spirits to the very highest quality. One of the partners in the business is the owner of a local farm and all the products at the distillery are made using Maine potatoes grown on the farm. These are perfect for production of high-quality vodka and gin, says the distillery. Unsurprisingly the water source is Maine's Cold River. The botanicals, including blueberries, are steeped before distillation, and each batch of gin is triple-distilled in a copper pot still before each bottle is hand-filled and numbered. Cold River prides itself on making a traditional style gin using seven botanicals.

Conncullin Gin

PRODUCER: Connacht Distillery

ABV: 47%

REGION AND COUNTRY OF ORIGIN: Mayo, Ireland

WEBSITE: www.connachtwhiskey.com

BOTANICALS: Juniper berries, elderberry flower, hawthorn berries

WHAT IT'S BEST SUITED TO: With redcurrants, a slice of Granny Smith apple, a Thomas Henry tonic, and plenty of ice.

The Connacht Distillery in Ballina, County Mayo stands next to the beautiful River Moy, famous the world over as a salmon river. The distillery was founded in 2015 by Irishman David Stapleton and his Irish-American cousins Robert Jensen, Robert Cassell, and PJ Stapleton. Their dream was to bring pure pot-still Irish whiskey back to the wild west of Ireland, with a view to exporting it to America. With the assistance of their friends, their dream became a reality. But they did not want to stop there, and now poitín, vodka, and gin are produced at the distillery. The distillery's statement gin, Conncullin, is named after the two lakes that provide the water for the distillery, Lough Conn and Lough Cullin. It serves as a metaphor for the Irish and Irish-Americans coming together as one.

Cotswolds Dry Gin

PRODUCER: The Cotswolds Distillery

ABV: 46%

REGION AND COUNTRY OF ORIGIN: Cotswolds, England

WEBSITE: www.cotswoldsdistillery.com

BOTANICALS: Juniper berries, angelica root, coriander, Cotswolds lavender and bay leaf, grapefruit, lime, black pepper, and cardamom seed

Right from the start The Cotswolds Distillery set out its stall, promising to make spirits of the highest quality, and it seems it is doing just that. The main spirit from the English distillery will be whisky, and it's still early days for the malt spirit. But the distillery's gin, beautifully packaged, of the highest quality, and with a distinctive Cotswolds twist, has won a strong following since it was launched. The distillery team reckon they're working in one of Britain's prettiest villages and they are determined to make a positive contribution to the community. So the small distillery has been designed to fit in with the landscape, and every step is taken to make sure production is environmentally friendly. Impressive and stylish.

Dà Mhìle Seaweed Gin

PRODUCER: Dà Mhìle

ABV: 42%

REGION AND COUNTRY OF ORIGIN: Ceredigian, Wales

WEBSITE: www.damhile.co.uk

BOTANICALS: Not distilled but including seaweed!

Dà Mhìle – pronounced Da-vee-lay – means 2000 and refers back to a project from 1992, when John Savage-Onstwedder, one of the founders of the renowned Teifi Farmhouse Cheese, and an organic farmer, commissioned the world-famous Springbank Distillery in Campbeltown, Scotland to produce the world's first organic whisky of the modern era, to commemorate the eagerly anticipated new millennium. John applied for a distiller's licence in 2010 and has been experimenting ever since. For this Dà Mhìle organic gin, seaweed from the local coast is infused over three weeks, giving it a greenish hue. The distillery makes food recommendations to accompany this uniquely Welsh product.

Daffy's Gin

PRODUCER: Daffy's

ABV: 43.4%

REGION AND COUNTRY OF ORIGIN: Scotland

WEBSITE: www.daffysgin.com

BOTANICALS: Juniper berries, Lebanese mint, coriander, angelica root, Spanish lemon, orange peel, cassia bark, orris root

Daffy is said to be the goddess of gin, and the makers of this Scottish gin are shooting high, describing it as the world's best gin. Certainly it has done extremely well since it was launched in 2014, with leading supermarkets and stylish High Street store Harvey Nichols stocking it very quickly. Its unique flavour comes from the inclusion of Lebanese mint as a botanical. The distillers say that great care was taken over the correct alcoholic strength, which was designed to balance the power of the spirit with the delicate and smooth mix of the botanicals. The bottle design – featuring Daffy – is the work of Robert McGinnis, an American artist who designed film posters for some of the James Bond films and classic films such as *Breakfast at Tiffany's.*

Darnley's View Spiced Gin

PRODUCER: Wemyss

ABV: 42.7%

REGION AND COUNTRY OF ORIGIN: Scotland

WEBSITE: www.darnleysview.com

BOTANICALS: Juniper berries, nutmeg, ginger, cumin, cinnamon, cassia, coriander seed, angelica root, cloves, grains of paradise

Since it was launched by independent whisky bottler Wemyss of Scotland, Darnley's View has gone from strength to strength. Named after the husband of Mary Queen of Scots, Darnley's View was made in London until 2017 when its owners announced the completion of a new gin distillery on the site of its Kingsbarns whisky distillery near St Andrew's as well as a whole image makeover for its range of gins. The new Darnley's Distillery is housed in a disused cottage and is set to provide an intriguing new visitor experience to add to Fife's flourishing food and drink tourism scene. This expression is said to be sparked by the Wemyss family's spirit of adventure. This gin uses a distinctive blend of ten botanicals including cloves, ginger, and grains of paradise. Contemporary in style, it is full and rounded with warm spice notes.

Death's Door

PRODUCER: Death's Door

ABV: 47%

REGION AND COUNTRY OF ORIGIN: Middleton, Wisconsin, USA

WEBSITE: www.deathsdoorspirits.com/spirits

BOTANICALS: Juniper berries, coriander, fennel

Death's Door Gin is part of a company that started life experimenting with agriculture and whether it could be sustained on the Wisconsin island of Washington, and is now an international business. The gin, based on the company's vodka, contains just three botanicals, but the distillery says that because of the distillation process it is able to keep all three balanced and making a significant taste contribution. At the core of this spirit are two strains of hard red winter wheat, which were cultivated to grow in the maritime climate of Washington island. So successful has the company been that it moved to a new distillery site in 2012, and can produce 250,000 cases of spirit a year.

Dingle Gin

PRODUCER: Dingle Distillery

ABV: 42.5%

REGION AND COUNTRY OF ORIGIN: Kerry, Ireland

WEBSITE: www.dingledistillery.ie/gin/

BOTANICALS: Mostly a secret, but including juniper berries, rowan berries, fucshia, bog myrtle, hawthorn, and heather

The Dingle Whiskey Distillery was established in November 2012, and prides itself on being a true artisan producer. It is not in the business of creating mega-brands, nor does it distil for anyone else. The distillery was also one of the first independent distilleries to start the new revolution of distilling in Ireland. While waiting for the whiskey, Dingle started making gin and vodka. Dingle was originally set up by Oliver Hughes, who sadly died suddenly, just before his whiskey came of age. Dingle distils gin, vodka, and whiskey in the charismatic town of Dingle, hidden behind the hills on the southwest coast of Ireland, next to the sea. The distillers say that the gin makes a great blackberry-and-thyme gin and tonic.

Dodd's Kew Organic Gin

PRODUCER: The London Distillery Company

ABV: 46%

REGION AND COUNTRY OF ORIGIN: London, England

WEBSITE: www.londondistillery.com/shop/
kew-organic-gin

BOTANICALS: Forty-two botanicals including juniper
berries, coriander seed, lemon peel, lime peel,
grapefruit peel, nutmeg, liquorice, cassia, santolina,
eucalyptus, rosemary, lemon grass, orris root, lavender

Dodd was a 19th-century entrepreneur who set up the
original London Distillery Company. The name was
adopted by Darren Rook when he set up a company
of the same name in Battersea in South London.
This gin is a collaboration with the nearby world-
famous Kew Royal Botanical Gardens and is made
using a whopping forty-two botanicals, some of
which come from the gardens. These are split into
four 'families' and infused for up to twenty-four hours,
before being distilled individually in the distillery's
pot still called Christina, before being blended and
bottled. The distillery says the finished gin is ideal for
a classic gin and tonic.

Dorothy Parker

PRODUCER: The New York Distilling Company

ABV: 46%

REGION AND COUNTRY OF ORIGIN: New York, USA

WEBSITE: www.nydistilling.com/spirits

BOTANICALS: A blend of traditional and contemporary botanicals, including juniper and elderberries, citrus, cinnamon, and hibiscus

The New York Distilling Company is a delightful mix of modern irreverence and fun, and serious and traditional drinks maker. Its navy strength gin is called Perry's Tot and is named after Matthew Perry, who served as commandant of the Brooklyn Naval Yard in the 1840s. This one is named after THAT Dorothy Parker.

'In an age of restless brilliance, Dorothy Parker was a singular sensation,' writes the company. 'A New Yorker at heart, her national celebrity sprang from her sharp, biting humour and widely quoted quips. An iconic enthusiast of gin and an unconventional woman, no one could have been a more interesting drinking companion.'

Fair enough. Sounds good enough to drink to.

Drumshanbo Gunpowder Gin

PRODUCER: The Shed Distillery

ABV: 43%

REGION AND COUNTRY OF ORIGIN: Leitrim, Ireland

WEBSITE: www. gunpowdergin.com

BOTANICALS: Juniper, Oriental lime, Oriental lemon, coriander, angelica root, caraway seed, star anise, meadowsweet, fresh grapefruit, cardamom, orris root, gunpowder tea

On the edge of a lake in Drumshanbo in the rural landscape in county Leitrim, PJ Rigney set up The Shed Distillery in 2015. It was romance that brought him there; it was where his parents first met. This gin helps to shine a light on an otherwise forgotten part of Ireland, and the distillery is using medieval copper pot stills in an attempt to bring something unique to an area that once had a vibrant distilling industry. Rigney makes an original and highly popular gin by mixing a taste of the Orient with that of Ireland. With its success he began exploring the areas of potato vodka, herbaceous gin liqueurs, and hand-crafted Irish whiskey. Try this gin with Licor 43, fresh mint, fresh apple, sugar syrup, and fresh lemon.

Dutch Courage Dry Gin

PRODUCER: Zuidam Distillery

ABV: 44.5%

REGION AND COUNTRY OF ORIGIN: Baarle-Nassau, Netherlands

BOTANICALS: Juniper berries, angelica root, cardamom, coriander seeds, lemon peel, liquorice root, orange peel, orris root, vanilla pod

The story goes that the expression 'Dutch courage' stems from the days when the English fought alongside the Dutch and drank genever before going into battle. It's possible that gin was originally invented in the Netherlands. Certainly there can be no doubt that the country has long produced a large number of exciting gin-related products. Zuidam is a highly impressive drinks maker with a history stretching back some fifty years. It produces hundreds of liqueurs, genevers, and spirits, including award-winning ryes and single malt whiskies, and is not scared to innovate and surprise. This is its take on the classic English gin style and, as with everything from the distillery, no shortcuts have been taken in its production.

DUTCH COURAGE

Dry Gin

Handcrafted
Small batch

BATCH NR.: 001
YEAR: 2015

1 LITER
44.5% ALC. BY VOL.

Zuidam Distillers
Baarle - Nassau, The Netherlands
Distilled from grain

East India Company London Dry Gin

PRODUCER: East India Company

ABV: 42%

REGION AND COUNTRY OF ORIGIN: London, England

WEBSITE: www.eic-gin.com

BOTANICALS: Not disclosed, but made with twelve botanicals, including juniper, coriander, angelica, liquorice, cocoa, and orris root

There are few companies with names more evocative than the East India Company. It conjures up history, adventure, and travel, as merchants established great trading routes and brought back tea, fruit, spices, and treasure. There are associations with Empire and the Raj, with great affluence and an other-worldly Britishness. It's an image that gin sits comfortably with, so when the new owners took over in 2005, they started researching the possibility of making a super premium gin. This is the result: a classic gin in a stylish bottle, with any number of nods to the company's past. The company says that the twelve botanicals are all linked to its own past and are sourced from countries linked to its trading past.

East London Liquor Premium Gin Batch No 1

PRODUCER: The East London Liquor Company

ABV: 45%

REGION AND COUNTRY OF ORIGIN: London, England

WEBSITE: www.eastlondonliquorcompany.com

BOTANICALS: Juniper berries, cassis bark, coriander seeds, angelica root, pink grapefruit peel, cubeb berries, Darjeeling tea

East London Liquor Company is a drinks hub operating on the site of an old glue factory in Bow Wharf, East London. The company, made up of a group of cool hipster youths who are fascinated by all things drink, has a distillery, a shop, and a bar, and imports all sorts of exotic hand-crafted spirits, including gin, vodka, rum, and whisky. The company is very proud that it is restoring distilling back to its East London roots for the first time in more than a century. The core gins were created with the help of renowned gin consultant Jamie Baxter, for this represents one of a limited number of special editions. They're an ambitious bunch, and are also making whisky. A taste of early spirit suggests that it will be every bit as good as this gin.

EAST
LONDON
LIQUOR COMPANY
LIMITED
Est. 2013
PREMIUM
GIN

BATCH
No.1

Infused with the finest botanicals.

JUNIPER BERRIES, CORIANDER SEEDS,
CASSIA BARK, ANGELICA ROOT,
DARJEELING TEA, PINK GRAPEFRUIT
PEEL, CUBEB BERRIES

45%VOL 70CLe

Eden Mill Love Gin

PRODUCER: Eden Mill Brewery

ABV: 42%

REGION AND COUNTRY OF ORIGIN: St Andrews, Scotland

WEBSITE: www.edenmill.com

BOTANICALS: Juniper berries, coriander seed, angelica, rhubarb root, rose petals, goji berries, elderberries, marshmallow root, raspberry leaves, hibiscus flowers

A glance through those botanicals explains how this gin comes to have a pink hue but, while the whole concept might seem a touch tacky and gimmicky, this is a serious offering from brewer turned distiller Eden Mill. The story goes that the team set themselves the task of creating an ideal Valentine's gift for February 14, 2015, and this is what they came up with. There's method to the pink-tinged madness, because the mix of fruit and flowers makes for a smooth, subtle, sophisticated gin with true élan. It can't hurt to get noticed in what is a very crowded field, either.

Edinburgh Gin

PRODUCER: Spencerfield Spirit Company

ABV: 43%

REGION AND COUNTRY OF ORIGIN: Edinburgh, Scotland

WEBSITE: www.edinburghgindistillery.co.uk

BOTANICALS: Thirteen botanicals, including juniper berries, angelica root, citrus peel, coriander seeds, orris root, heather, and milk thistle

There's something very special about the Edinburgh Distillery, which is underground, right in the heart of Edinburgh. Its owners describe it as being in a rabbit hole. It's in the heart of Scotland's capital that a range of gins and gin liqueurs are put together, including a very special navy strength gin by the name of Cannonball. This is the more standard offering and is a solid and well-made gin. The distillery welcomes visitors and offers tours, and you can try your hand at making gin while visiting. Proof that Scottish gin can be every bit as classy as a single-malt whisky.

Fifty Pounds Gin

PRODUCER: Thames Distillers

ABV: 44%

REGION AND COUNTRY OF ORIGIN: London, England

WEBSITE: www.fiftypoundsgin.co.uk

BOTANICALS: Eleven botanicals, including juniper berries, angelica root, coriander seeds, grains of paradise, lemon peel, liquorice root, orange peel

The gin's name refers to the punitive levy introduced by the Gin Act of 1736, which marked the beginning of the end for England's raucous and damaging love affair with gin. The producers claim that at that time a special gin was created to a recipe and was referred to as 'Fifty Pounds Gin'. That gin recipe was rediscovered and is re-created in this bottling. Fifty Pounds is produced in a small distillery in Southeast London, and the gin is distilled four times, using a traditional distilling method, to produce a sophisticated, smooth, and pleasant traditional London Gin.

Filliers Dry Gin Tangerine

PRODUCER: Filliers

ABV: 44%

REGION AND COUNTRY OF ORIGIN: Belgium

WEBSITE: www.filliersdrygin28.com

BOTANICALS: Twenty-eight botanicals, including juniper berries, coriander seeds, lavender flowers, orange blossom, allspice, malt, bitter root, ginger, mandarins

This is a Belgian gin and therefore is closely linked to the natural Belgian heritage of genever. The spirit it is based on, Filliers 28, is made up of 28 botanicals, and the recipe was created by Firmin Filliers, a third-generation master distiller of the Filliers family, shortly after the end of the First World War in 1918. It was made in small batches in a distillery dating back to 1880, on a small alembic still. For this gin, an extension of the original, premium mandarin oranges from the Valencia region of Spain are used – despite the gin's name.

'They are the fruit of an exclusive course of sunshine therapy enjoyed between November and January, carefully selected for their beauty, freshness, and flavour,' says the distillery.

The gin is distilled five times in traditional copper pot stills.

Finsbury Platinum

PRODUCER: Finsbury Distillery

ABV: 47%

REGION AND COUNTRY OF ORIGIN: London, England

BOTANICALS: Undisclosed, but including juniper berries, coriander seeds, lemon peel, orange peel, angelica, lime zest, ginger, iris, almond

One of gin's more esoteric and mysterious expressions, Finsbury Platinum can trace its history back to 1740, and its recipe has been a closely guarded secret ever since, though exotic fruits and spices are included in its make-up. This is a high-alcohol gin, and the juniper and citrus content features prominently. The name deliberately associates the gin with London. It is traditional in style, but information on its heritage and history is sketchy. These days it sells into international markets and especially Germany, where it is one of the leading brands. But some bartenders love it because of its bold flavours.

Flemish OriGIN

PRODUCER: Stokerij De Moor

ABV: 49.3%

REGION AND COUNTRY OF ORIGIN: Aalst, Belgium

WEBSITE: www.flemishgin.com

BOTANICALS: Juniper berries, cubeb pepper, ginger root, clove, cinnamon, cardamom, grains of paradise, nutmeg, lemon peel, star anise, cassis, rosemary, orange peel, coriander seeds, liquorice, orris root, yarrow, hops, gentian root, angelica, carob, lavender blossom, blessed thistle

Another gin from Belgium. This one is from a distillery known for its genevers and liqueurs. Its main gin, called Gin 20-3, is produced in small batches of between two hundred and two hundred and fifty litres on a traditional copper pot still, and each bottle is filled, closed, and labelled by hand. This version is even more select. During the distillation process of FG 20-3, four or five very small 'cuts' are taken, at times when certain flavours are considered to be at their maximum. These small quantities are blended together from the very heart cut of the distillate. This makes up a total of about twenty-five litres per batch, or a mere thirty-five to thirty-six hand-numbered bottles.

Fords

PRODUCER: The 86 Co

ABV: 45%

REGION AND COUNTRY OF ORIGIN: London, England

WEBSITE: www.fordsgin.com

BOTANICALS: Juniper berries, coriander seed, lemon peel, bitter orange peel, jasmine, orris powder, cassia, grapefruit peel, angelica

Fords comes with a substantial pedigree. It is a collaboration between highly skilled distiller Charles Maxwell of Thames Distillers and former Beefeater and Plymouth Gin brand ambassador Simon Ford, who knows a thing or two about gin. The botanicals here are steeped for fifteen hours before distillation in a 500-litre still. The idea behind this gin is to keep the traditional juniper flavour to the fore, but to soften it with strong citrus flavours, making the gin perfect for gin and tonics but also for martinis. The gin is bottled in California using local well water. This is bottled at a weighty 45% ABV and has an attractive oiliness to it. Well worth seeking out.

G'Vine Floraison

PRODUCER: G'Vine Gin

ABV: 40%

REGION AND COUNTRY OF ORIGIN: Cognac, France

WEBSITE: g-vine.com/our-gins/

BOTANICALS: Juniper berries, ginger roots, green cardamom, liquorice, lime peel, cassia bark, coriander, cubeb berries, nutmeg, vine flowers

This is a French gin with its roots in Cognac, a region obviously renowned for its high-quality grapes and, sure enough, grapes are at the base of the spirit used here. There are two sister gins from the distillery, with this one using vine flowers that only bloom for a few days a year. The botanicals are put into groups and macerated and distilled before blending. The sister gin, called Nouaison, has a higher alcoholic strength. It is drier and contains the small berries that grow on the vine after flowering. Both versions are distilled four times in a small copper still before the vine flowers are added and a further distillation takes place. Both are stylish, complex, fragrant gins.

Gilpin's

PRODUCER: Thames Distillers

ABV: 47%

REGION AND COUNTRY OF ORIGIN: London, England

WEBSITE: www.gilpinsgin.com

BOTANICALS: Juniper berries, bitter orange, sage, borage, lime peel, lemon peel, coriander, angelica root

Matthew Gilpin knew exactly what he wanted when he created his gin – a spirit that would revel in its Englishness while showcasing two of his favourite herbs, sage and borage. And he has achieved his aim in bucket loads with this stylish and ever-so-dry London-style gin. Gilpin's contains eight botanicals and is, in the main, a traditional gin, but the herbal notes and a lack of sweet botanicals make this an extra-dry offering and with the weighty alcoholic strength, it works beautifully. This is made using spring water from the Lake District – a link to an 800-year-old story in which a ferocious wild boar which terrorized pilgrims in the region was defeated by Richard 'the Rider' de Gilpin, and the wild boar was granted as a symbol for the Gilpin family. You'll find it on the label.

Gin Mare

PRODUCER: Gin Mare

ABV: 42.7%

REGION AND COUNTRY OF ORIGIN: Spain

WEBSITE: www.ginmare.es

BOTANICALS: Juniper berries, coriander, Arbequina olives, green cardamom, citrus fruits, thyme, basil, rosemary

This Spanish gin was intended to be different from the outset and, thanks to the inclusion of olives and a group of assertive herbs, it is. The idea behind it was to create a distinctly Mediterranean gin. Made in an ancient fishing village lying between the Costa Brava and the Costa Dorada, the gin is based on a spirit made from barley. The botanicals are macerated and distilled separately or in small groupings, with some requiring a maceration process of a year. The six resulting distillates are then blended together. Purists won't like it, as juniper doesn't make all the running, but it's a distinctive, different, and very well-made spirit that ticks all the right boxes when mixed with tonic or used in a martini.

Colección de au

GIN MAR

ISTILLED FROM OLIVES, THYME, ROSEMARY

700 ml. Alc.42.7% vol.

Ginerosity

PRODUCER: Ginerosity

ABV: 40%

REGION AND COUNTRY OF ORIGIN: Edinburgh, Scotland

WEBSITE: www.ginerosity.com

BOTANICALS: Juniper berries, coriander, angelica, lemon, lime, orange, lemon myrtle, heather, cardamom, cloves

The name is a bit gimmicky and suggests that there's more to this gin than a few botanicals. Let's deal with the gin itself, first, though. Made by Pickering's at Summerhall Distillery, this a well-made, stylish Scottish gin made with ten botanicals. But a clue to what makes this gin stand out is contained in the name. Purchase a bottle and all the profits from it are poured back into projects that will help deserving young adults to build themselves a better future.

'That isn't just a worthwhile cause, it's a vital one,' say the five-person team behind the idea. 'And we're exceptionally proud that we're the first spirits company to do it.'

Ginerosity has linked up with the charity Challenges Worldwide to help young adults from disadvantaged backgrounds take part in International Citizenship Service (ICS) programmes.

Glendalough Wild Botanical Gin

PRODUCER: Glendalough Distillery

ABV: 42%

REGION AND COUNTRY OF ORIGIN: Wicklow, Ireland.

WEBSITE: www.glendaloughdistillery.com/our-gin

BOTANICALS: Freshly foraged botanicals for each batch

Founded in the summer of 2014, Glendalough is part of a revival of the distilling heritage Ireland once had. It was set up by five friends from Dublin and Wicklow, whose idea was to make innovative spirits while staying true to tradition. Set within what is known as 'The Garden of Ireland', the distillery has access to some of the best ingredients anyone could wish for for making gin. Teaming up with friends Geraldine Kavanagh and distiller Rowdy Rooney, they set about making their dream a reality. They started off making a range of poitíns. From there they moved into whiskey and seasonal gins, while recognizing the need for a standard Glendalough gin. This resulted in Wild Botanical Gin, released in early 2017. This gin represents a labour of love and passion that has built quite the following at home and abroad.

WILD
IRISH
GIN

GLENDALOUGH

WILD B☐+∆NICAL GIN

41%Vol HAND CRAFTED IN SMALL BATCHES WITH FRESH 700ml
WILD FLORA FROM THE WICKLOW MOUNTAINS

Gordon's Export

PRODUCER: Diageo

ABV: 47.3%

REGION AND COUNTRY OF ORIGIN: Fife, Scotland

WEBSITE: www.gordonsgin.com

BOTANICALS: Not disclosed

The standard Gordon's gin is, of course, sold in the famous green bottle and is one of the world's most recognizable drinks brands. This, the export version, contains exactly the same gin, but has an alcoholic content of 47.3%, compared with the standard version of just 37.5%. This has an altogether fruitier, fresher, and fuller taste. Gordon's has a history going back to 1769, when Alexander Gordon started producing a London Dry Gin in South London. Today it is made in Scotland by drinks giant Diageo at its grain distillery Cameronbridge. Described as 'the ginniest of all gins', this has a bold and assertive juniper taste, but this version also has a strong citric theme and a pleasant spicy one.

THE ORIGINAL

GORDON'S

LONDON DRY GIN

DISTILLED IN GREAT BRITAIN

ESTD 1769

ALEXANDER GORDON & COMPANY

IMPORTED

DISTILLED TO THE ORIGINAL SECRET
RECIPE OF ALEXANDER GORDON

40% vol   70 cl

Greenall's Original

PRODUCER: Greenall's

ABV: 40%

REGION AND COUNTRY OF ORIGIN: Warrington, England

WEBSITE: www.greenallsgin.com

BOTANICALS: Seven undisclosed botanicals, including juniper berries, coriander, Spanish lemons, and angelica root

Greenall's is a highly successful brewer operating in the northwest of England, but it has had interests elsewhere for a long time, and it takes its distilling operation very seriously indeed, distilling its own spirits and making spirits for other companies. The distillery in Warrington was founded in 1761 by Thomas Dakin and a version of what is now known as Greenall's Original has been made on the site for more than two hundred and fifty years. The current master distiller, Joanne Moore, has been with Greenall's for more than twenty years. Greenall's also makes a sloe gin and a wild berry gin.

Hayman's Royal Dock

PRODUCER: Anno Distillers

ABV: 57%

REGION AND COUNTRY OF ORIGIN: Witham, England

WEBSITE: www.haymansgin.com

BOTANICALS: Juniper berries, coriander, lemon peel, orange peel, angelica, orris root, cinnamon, cassia bark, nutmeg, liquorice

Hayman's makes traditional London Dry Gin at its distillery in Essex and prides itself on its attention to detail. All the botanicals are measured by hand and are then steeped in English wheat spirit for a full day prior to distillation, which allows the oils and essences to infuse fully. Royal Dock uses the same botanicals as London Dry Gin but in different proportions. It is also bottled at navy strength of 57% – the strength at which gunpowder will still light when it is soaked in spirit, a measure to ensure that spirit provided to the navy wasn't watered down by unscrupulous drinks merchants. An outstanding gin, beautifully made.

ROYAL DOCK
of Deptford

NAVY STRENGTH
GIN

*Provisioner to the Admiralty
and trade from 1863*

57% VOL.　　HAYMAN DISTILLERS
ENGLAND　　70cl

FAMILY GIN
DISTILLERS
SINCE 1863
ENGLAND

Hendrick's

PRODUCER: William Grant & Sons

ABV: 41.4%

REGION AND COUNTRY OF ORIGIN: Girvan, Scotland

WEBSITE: us.hendricksgin.com

BOTANICALS: Juniper berries, yarrow, elderflower, angelica root, orange peel, caraway seeds, camomile, cubeb berries, coriander, orris root, lemon, rose, cucumber

While Bombay Sapphire can take much of the credit for bringing gin in from the cold, Hendrick's played a key role in the drink's rehabilitation. It's owned by William Grant & Sons, a Scottish family-owned company that you'd expect to be stuffy and old-fashioned but that is anything but. With Monkey Shoulder blended malt whisky playing a similar role for Scotch whisky, Hendrick's was targeted at the trendy cocktail set and, backed by an ultracool website, it set about bringing a steampunk mentality to the drink. It's flavoured with rose and cucumber post distillation and new drinkers were won over by a constant supply of new drink serves. Classy.

Hernö

PRODUCER: Hernö Gin

ABV: 40.5%

REGION AND COUNTRY OF ORIGIN: Härnösand, Sweden

WEBSITE: www.hernogin.com

BOTANICALS: Juniper berries, coriander, fresh lemon peel, Swedish lingonberries, meadowsweet, black pepper, cassia, vanilla

Hernö is a Swedish distillery founded by John Hillgren, who got a taste for gin while working in London in the late 1990s. The distillery is in an area of outstanding natural beauty and was Sweden's first gin distillery when it was set up in 2011. Just as is the case with Swedish whisky, this gin is excellently made and Hillgren has hit on a unique and niche taste profile that has won this gin countless awards, including top honours at the International Wine and Spirit Competition. The distillery also makes a cask gin, a navy strength one, and its own version of Old Tom. This, though, is a good place to start.

Hibernation

PRODUCER: Dyfi Distillery

ABV: 45%

REGION AND COUNTRY OF ORIGIN: Wales

WEBSITE: www.dyfidistillery.com

BOTANICALS: Juniper berries, cassia bark, angelica, lemon, liquorice, coriander seed, orris, crab apples, blackberries, bilberries, lingonberries

Dyfi Distillery is a small family distillery in Wales that is bringing something of a scientific approach to its products. Hibernation Gin is the most innovative of its gins, and its least conventional. The distillery is located in an old slate-mining village and botanicals are sourced locally before being distilled on two 100-litre stills. Only one distillation is done each week at most, and this is only distilled in late autumn, when the special botanicals are available. Once distilled, the gin is stored in white port casks, which gives it a unique flavour. In April 2017 *The Independent* chose it as its Best Buy new gin. The distillers say that it can be served as a sipping gin but that it also makes an excellent negroni.

HMS Victory Navy Strength

PRODUCER: Isle of Wight Distillery

ABV: 57%

REGION AND COUNTRY OF ORIGIN: Isle of Wight, England

WEBSITE: www.isleofwightdistillery.com

BOTANICALS: Not disclosed, but including juniper berries, grains of paradise and citrus peel

This gin is made by the Isle of Wight Distillery, which was founded in 2015 by Xavier Baker and Conrad Gauntlett. Such was its success that by the summer of 2017 the ever-growing operation had moved to its permanent home on Pondwell Hill, Ryde. HMS Victory gin is made in partnership with the National Museum of the Royal Navy. Victory attempts to re-create the style of gin drunk by naval officers during the Battle of Trafalgar. The gin is aged in casks containing some wood from *HMS Victory* itself, and a portion of the profits have gone to fund the ongoing restoration of the famous old ship. The distillers say that Victory tastes particularly good with ice-cold tonic, slices of pink grapefruit, and plenty of ice.

Hoxton

PRODUCER: Gerry Calabrese

ABV: 40%

REGION AND COUNTRY OF ORIGIN: London, England

WEBSITE: www.hoxtongin.com

BOTANICALS: Undisclosed, but including juniper berries, iris, tarragon, ginger, coconut, pink grapefruit

When the debate over what constitutes a gin and what doesn't comes up, and it does regularly, chances are Hoxton Gin will be included in the conversation. No gin tests 'predominantly juniper' requirement more than this one, with coconut very much to the fore. That aside, though, there's a lot to be said for this spirit, which is named after one of London's most established creative hubs and has been put together by highly acclaimed mixologist, writer, and drinks consultant, Gerry Calabrese. The botanicals are macerated for five days and then distilled once in a 150-year-old copper still. Coconut and grapefruit are added and the spirit is then rested for two months in steel tanks. A range of exciting cocktail ideas by Calabrese can be found on the website.

Inverroche Classic

PRODUCER: Inverroche Distillery

ABV: 43%

REGION AND COUNTRY OF ORIGIN: Stillbay, South Africa

WEBSITE: www.inverroche.co.za

BOTANICALS: Juniper berries, citrus peel, angelica root, cassia bark, coriander seed, cardamom, various Cape Fynbos flowers and plants

Inverroche Distillery is situated in a region of huge natural importance and historical significance in South Africa. The distillers put a great deal of emphasis on the special local flora and fauna and incorporate them into its spirits. Not far from the distillery are caves that may have offered shelter to early humans 195,000 years ago, when a devastating ice age nearly wiped life out altogether, and again 100,000 years ago, as the era of modern man was starting. The region is rich in unique plant and flower life. This gin is distilled in a 1,000-litre flexible wood-fired copper pot still called Meg, designed specially for the distillery by a family of coppersmiths from Stellenbosch.

inverroche

GIN CLASSIC

inverroche

— SMALL BATCH DISTILLED —

GIN
CLASSIC

HANDCRAFTED
WITH WILD CAPE FYNBOS
BOTANICALS

Distilled and bottled in South Africa

Japanese Gin

PRODUCER: The Cambridge Distillery

ABV: 42%

REGION AND COUNTRY OF ORIGIN: Cambridge, England

WEBSITE: www.cambridgedistillery.co.uk

BOTANICALS: Juniper berries, shiso leaf, sesame seeds, cucumber, sanshō, yuzo

'London meets Tokyo' it says on the website, but that's not entirely accurate, because this is actually made at The Cambridge Distillery, where they're prepared to turn their hands to all sorts of interesting concoctions. Here the distillery has taken a traditional London Gin recipe and combined it with Japanese botanicals, including shiso leaf, which is a culinary herb, sanshō, which is a distinctive spice, and yuzo, which provides a citrus zest flavour. Each botanical is individually distilled by hand, under vacuum, in tiny volumes, before being blended. The distillery uses low-temperature distillation to capture the freshest possible flavours.

Jensen's Bermondsey Gin

PRODUCER: Christian Jensen

ABV: 43%

REGION AND COUNTRY OF ORIGIN: London, England

WEBSITE: www.bermondseygin.com

BOTANICALS: Undisclosed

'There's really nothing new about Jensen's,' states the distillery's website, and then adds, 'and that's why it's different.' In today's crowded gin market that statement's not entirely correct any more, but when you consider some of the more extreme and ludicrous attempts to dig up a unique selling point, there's something very refreshing about a distiller who is obsessed with creating the finest traditional London Dry Gin, faithfully attempting to re-create the flavours of London's lost distilleries. Christian Jensen started making gin in 2004 and now has his own distillery close to the Thames, in fashionable Bermondsey. His gin is distilled in small batches. This, he says, is how gin should be. The distillery also makes a version of Old Tom.

jensen's

When Christian Jensen
first tasted the vintage
gins from London's lost
distilleries, he began
a journey. Creating a
finely balanced gin that
honoured these forgotten
recipes became his
obsession. That's why
Jensen's is distilled in
small batches, using only
traditional gin botanicals.
So there's really nothing
new about Jensen's, and
that's why it's different.
Distilled in Bermondsey,
London, Jensen's is gin as
it was. Gin as it should be.

LONDON DISTILLED
BERMONDSEY DRY GIN

70CL 43% VOL.

Junipero Gin

PRODUCER: Anchor Distilling

ABV: 49.3%

REGION AND COUNTRY OF ORIGIN: San Francisco, USA

WEBSITE: www.anchordistilling.com/junipero

BOTANICALS: Undisclosed

Anchor Distilling was way ahead of the curve when it came to both craft distilling and re-creating historical recipes. The distillery started making all sorts of forgotten distillates in 1996, including highly unusual and much-sought-after 100% rye whiskeys. This is a juniper-rich gin containing at least twelve botanicals. The distillery says that it gained the skill of mixing herbs, spices, and botanicals from making Anchor Brewing Company's annual Christmas Ale for ten years. This is a distinctive and complex gin, which the distillery says is bottled at a weighty 49.3% ABV because it makes it ideal for mixing into a range of cocktail drinks.

Ki No Bi Gin

PRODUCER: Kyoto Distillery

ABV: 45.7%

REGION AND COUNTRY OF ORIGIN: Kyoto, Japan

WEBSITE: www.kyotodistillery.jp

BOTANICALS: Juniper berries, orris, hinoki, yuzu, lemon, green tea, ginger, red shiso leaves, bamboo leaves, sanshō pepper, kinome

The Cambridge Distillery in England may have produced the first Japanese-style gin, but this is the first gin to be distilled in Kyoto. Everything about this screams elegance and style, including the enticing and complex taste. Ki No Bi has a rice spirit base and is made with water sourced from the famous sake-making region of Fushimi. To make it, the botanicals are divided into six categories – base, citrus, tea, herbal, spice, and floral – and are distilled separately. The key to this gin lies with the hinoki (cypress) wood chips, bamboo, and gyokuro tea, which give the gin a herbal earthiness, and the green sanshō (peppercorns) and ginger, which provide spice.

Kirsty's Gin

PRODUCER: Arbikie Highland Estate

ABV: 43%

REGION AND COUNTRY OF ORIGIN: Angus, Scotland

WEBSITE: www.arbikie.com

BOTANICALS: Juniper berries, kelp, carline thistle, blaeberries

The Stirling family have been farmers in Scotland for generations, having farmed the Arbikie Highland estate since the 1920s. Today the farm, which lies on Scotland's east coast, is in the hands of brothers John, Iain, and David. They proudly maintain that they use grain grown on the estate and produce their two gins with local botanicals. Kirsty's Gin is named after master distiller Kirsty Black. This version uses local kelp and blueberries. Sister gin, AK's, is made with wheat, honey, black pepper, mace, and cardamom. The distillery also produces vodka and is maturing whisky spirit, using red wine casks as well as the more traditional ex-sherry and ex-bourbon ones.

Langton's No 1

PRODUCER: Greenalls

ABV: 40%

REGION AND COUNTRY OF ORIGIN: Warrington, England

WEBSITE: www.langtonsgin.co.uk

BOTANICALS: Twelve botanicals, including juniper berries, lemon peel, orange peel, liquorice, Lake District oak bark, Lakeland botanicals

Although Langton's No 1 isn't produced in the Lake District in the northwest of England, its owners go to considerable lengths to make it with Lakeland ingredients. The water is sourced from a borehole under Skiddaw, a mountain in the region, and may well have spent centuries making its way to the surface through slate, giving the distillery licence to describe as 'slate-filtered water'. The bottle itself is cleverly based on the contours of a piece of slate. The overall taste isn't conventional at all, and juniper flavours are ordered, rather than dominant. But this is balanced, and as it's distilled four times, it's smooth, rounded, and with a pleasant herbal note.

Listoke 1777

PRODUCER: Listoke Distillery

ABV: 43.3%

REGION AND COUNTRY OF ORIGIN: Louth, Ireland

WEBSITE: www.listokedistillery.ie

BOTANICALS: Juniper berries, coriander, angelica root, and six others

Opened in August 2016, the Listoke Distillery lies just outside the city of Drogheda, nestled in the Boyne Valley in County Louth, some forty minutes from Dublin. The distillery, set up by Raymond and Juliet Gogan, is sited inside a two hundred-year-old stable, once a home to barn owls. It is arguably the most modern distillery in Ireland. The distillery sits on the grounds of the beautiful Listoke estate, where the distillery team gathers some special ingredients for its 1777 gin. The gin is distilled, blended, and bottled on site. The couple have also set up Ireland's first gin school, so interested parties can sign up to capture the truly rare experience of making gin in the twenty-first century. The 1777 refers to the year Scotch whisky was sent over to England, and when Listoke House was literally put on the map, with the publication of the first map of Ireland.

Liverpool Gin

PRODUCER: Halewood International

ABV: 42%

REGION AND COUNTRY OF ORIGIN: Liverpool, England

WEBSITE: www.liverpoolgin.com

BOTANICALS: Undisclosed

English gin has always had a special link to the sea, and busy port cities such as Bristol, Plymouth, and Liverpool had gins based on the botanicals that were flowing through the docks. Liverpool Gin, created by Mark Hensby, who owns the Liverpool Organic Brewery, and Belvedere pub licensee John O'Dowd in 2012, is an attempt to re-create some of the original Liverpool-style gin. The gin was originally targeted at high-end retail outlets, and there is a strong Spanish link to the brand, but it is currently in a state of flux having been bought by Harewood International in 2016. There are ambitious export plans for it in the coming months. There is a Valencian orange and rose version of the gin. One to watch in the coming months.

London Hill

PRODUCER: Langley distillery

ABV: 40%

REGION AND COUNTRY OF ORIGIN: West Midlands, England

WEBSITE: www.ianmacleod.com/brands/london-hill-gin

BOTANICALS: Twelve botanicals, including juniper berries, lemon peel, sweet orange peel, and coriander seeds

The owner of London Hill Gin is Scottish drinks company Ian Macleod, an independent bottler, and owner of the Glengoyne and Tamdhu malt whisky distilleries. The company also has a managing director who knows a thing or two about gin, so you'd expect this to be good – and it is. It's produced at the Langley distillery in the English West Midlands (home of Broker's Gin) and you don't see it very often, which is a shame. It's made to a traditional recipe and it's refreshing, flavoursome, and punchy. In recent years it has been repackaged and repositioned as a more premium gin – with limited success.

Makar Glasgow Gin

PRODUCER: The Glasgow Distillery Company

ABV: 43%

REGION AND COUNTRY OF ORIGIN: Glasgow, Scotland

WEBSITE: www.glasgowdistillery.com

BOTANICALS: Not disclosed

The Glasgow Distillery Company was the first whisky producer in the city for more than a century. It not only went all out to be able to claim that honour, it didn't muck about when it came to producing fine spirit. The distillery is sizeable and the three founders make for a highly impressive management team. They have installed top-quality distilling equipment, have sourced a substantial number of top-quality casks, and have appointed outstanding distillers. Whisky is still some time off but its first product was Makar Gin, and it immediately set about picking up awards. The distillery also does an Old Tom, aged, and flavoured gins. Very impressive early days indeed.

Martin Miller's Westbourne Strength

PRODUCER: Langley Distillery

ABV: 45.2%

REGION AND COUNTRY OF ORIGIN: West Midlands, England

WEBSITE: www.martinmillersgin.com

BOTANICALS: Juniper berries, cassia, coriander, nutmeg, bitter orange peel, dried lime peel, dried lemon peel, orris root, angelica root, liquorice root, cucumber essence

Martin Miller's is made by Langley Distillery in the West Midlands for a company formed by the late Martin Miller, who started experimenting with craft gin in 1999, way before the gin revolution of the early Millennium. Miller was exploring what happened when he distilled Icelandic water, which he considered the purest in the world, with the essence of cucumber. His aim was to maintain the traditional but also be innovative. Westbourne Strength is made to the recipe on the same still and with the same Icelandic water as the original gin, but the higher strength intensifies both juniper and citrus components, making for a more traditional gin and one that works well with tonic, in a negroni, or as a cocktail ingredient.

Mascaró Gin 9

PRODUCER: Mascaró family

ABV: 40%

REGION AND COUNTRY OF ORIGIN: Vilafranca del Penèdes, Spain

WEBSITE: www.mascaro.es/en/distilled/gin9

BOTANICALS: Not disclosed, but lots of juniper berries

Mascaró is a company based about fifty kilometres from Barcelona, which has been producing a wide range of alcoholic products for three generations. It makes everything from wine and cavas to orange liqueurs, and it prides itself on applying the highest standards to its distillates, which include brandy and gin. This particular gin is the creation of Antonio Mascaró, and it stays close to a traditional London Gin style recipe as it can. But the gin is surprisingly light and fresh too, with a nice clean taste that no doubt goes well with chilled tonic and ice on those glorious Spanish evenings.

Mombasa Club

PRODUCER: Thames Distillers

ABV: 41.5%

REGION AND COUNTRY OF ORIGIN: London, England

BOTANICALS: Juniper berries, angelica root, coriander seed, cassia bark, cumin, clove

The Mombasa Club was a British-only club on Africa's East Coast that during the days of the Empire played a crucial part in Colonial life. Mombasa had become an important trading centre, lying opposite Zanzibar, which was strategically placed to become a commercial hub and major port. Mombasa was where the Colony met wild Africa, with all the drama and excitement that would have meant. Members of the Mombasa Club would have debated the news and planned strategies while drinking a local gin. This version is spicy, to represent the spices on offer from Zanzibar, and is made in London by Thames Distillers. Cloves and cumin are among the ingredients in a gin that casts an affectionate eye to a long-lost era.

Monkey 47 Schwarzwald Dry Gin

PRODUCER: Black Forest Distillers

ABV: 47%

REGION AND COUNTRY OF ORIGIN: Black Forest, Germany

WEBSITE: www.monkey47.com

BOTANICALS: Juniper berries, elderberry, allspice, honey pomelo, English hawthorn, cloves, blackberry, orange liquorice, true sage, acacia flowers, ginger, jasmine, angelica, camomile, the gardener's hope, the musketeer, rosehip, nutmeg, the marshmallow man, common vervain, grains of paradise, coriander, scarlet monarda, spruce shoots

Take a look at the list of botanicals in this gin, and it's tempting to think this is made by German distillers with a very good sense of humour. Check the website, though, and you can find all you want to know about the botanicals here. This isn't so much as a horticultural and home science course. Unsurprisingly, this is complex but a great deal of fun. It's said to be based on an old recipe for a gin made by the owner of a Black Forest guest house called The Wild Monkey. The website is home to The Monkey Drum, and once you get past the text-heavy pages, there's a pleasant and relaxing humour running through it. It's the perfect accompaniment for this unique gin.

No 3 Gin

PRODUCER: Under licence for Berry Bros & Rudd

ABV: 46%

REGION AND COUNTRY OF ORIGIN: Holland

WEBSITE: www.no3gin.com

BOTANICALS: Juniper berries, angelica root, coriander seed, sweet orange peel, cardamom seeds, grapefruit peel

This is distilled to a specific recipe containing just six botanicals for Berry, Bros & Rudd, the Mayfair fine wine and spirits retailers who have operated at No 3 James Street since 1698. This was the luxury end of the drinks market, and the great and the good would buy their fine wines and other luxuries while getting themselves weighed in the store. A visit today is a fascinating glance into another era so, unsurprisingly, we're talking about a stylish and elegant gin here. But for all the stylish tradition, there's a hint of modernity and innovation with the use of grapefruit. Berry, Bros & Rudd have teamed up with a Dutch family producer with more than three hundred years' distilling experience – perfect for such a prestigious spirits retailer.

Nolet's

PRODUCER: The Nolet family

ABV: 47.6%

REGION AND COUNTRY OF ORIGIN: Schiedam, Netherlands

WEBSITE: www.noletsgin.com

BOTANICALS: Juniper berries, lemon peel, orris root, liquorice root, orange peel, white peach, Turkish rose, raspberry

The bottle and the smart pictures of the members of the Nolet family on the website suggest a formal, old-fashioned approach to spirits making, and with ten generations of distilling experience for this Dutch family concern, it would make total sense if this was an operation steeped in history. It's not. Current Nolet distillers Carl Jr and Bob worked closely with their father Carolus Sr to create this, but this is anything but a traditional gin. It bursts with fruit flavours and floral notes, and has rose, raspberry, and white peach in its make-up. The result is a stylish, modern, unique, and even feminine nature to it. Doesn't hold up well to being mixed, though. Not for everybody, but there may just be a whole world of non gin lovers who'd adore this.

Old Raj

PRODUCER: Hayman's for Cadenhead's

ABV: 55%

REGION AND COUNTRY OF ORIGIN: Essex, England

WEBSITE: www.wmcadenhead.com

BOTANICALS: Juniper, coriander, Seville orange peel, lemon peel, liquorice, angelica root, orris, cinnamon, cassia quills, nutmeg, plus a little post-distillation saffron

Another gin with a name harking back to the days of Empire, this was made at Springbank Distillery on the west coast of Scotland but is now made by Hayman's at its distillery in Essex, England. That in itself is a statement of quality. The spirit is distilled in England but it is transported to William Cadenhead, where it is bottled at three different strengths. Two of the gins, including this one, also have saffron added post distillation. Old Raj is bottled at 55%, making it an early example of craft distilling. Cadenhead's argues that by holding prices down despite its cult status and premium reputation, its high quality but moderate price ensure its future way beyond when the fad for craft gin wanes.

Opihr Oriental Spiced

PRODUCER: Greenall's

ABV: 40%

REGION AND COUNTRY OF ORIGIN: Warrington, England

WEBSITE: www.opihr.com

BOTANICALS: Not disclosed, but including juniper berries, cubeb berries, Tellicherry black pepper, cumin, coriander, orange peel, and grapefruit peel

If you want to get a sense of just how far some gin makers go to source botanicals, take a look at the excellent website of Opihr. Through a map it takes you on a journey around the world collecting the botanicals to make this, the spiciest, fruitiest gin you'll ever taste. The whole point of this gin is to pay tribute to the spice route. The words 'Oriental' and 'Spiced' are appropriate because this smells like a cross between the Chinese curry sauce you get in fish-and-chip shops and creamy korma curry. The name itself is taken from a legendary region that blossomed at the time of King Solomon, apparently.

Oxley

PRODUCER: Thames Distillers for Bacardi

ABV: 47%

REGION AND COUNTRY OF ORIGIN: London, England

WEBSITE: www.oxleygin.com

BOTANICALS: Fourteen botanicals, not disclosed, but including juniper berries, angelica root, orris root, fresh orange peel, fresh lemon peel, fresh grapefruit peel, cassia bark, vanilla, meadowsweet, aniseed

This is arguably one of the most innovative gins on the market, made by Thames Distillers under special conditions on behalf of Oxley's owners, Bacardi. The owners took years to settle on the final botanicals, and the distillation process is pretty much the opposite of most gins, with the botanicals distilled together at sub-zero temperatures and under pressure, so that the flavour compounds are infused by chill, not heat. If this fascinates you, then there are several geeky websites that will attempt to take you through the process in depth, though their communication skills leave much to be desired.

What's important here, though, is, is it any good? The answer's yes.

Pickering's

PRODUCER: Summerhall Distillery

ABV: 42%

REGION AND COUNTRY OF ORIGIN: Edinburgh, Scotland

WEBSITE: www.pickeringsgin.com

BOTANICALS: Juniper berries, coriander, cardamom, angelica, fennel, anise, lemon, lime, cloves

Summerhall Distillery has been making gin since 2004, so it precedes the current craft distilling boom, but there's nothing very conventional about it. It operates out of an old animal hospital, which was part of a veterinary school known locally as The Dick Vet. Now it's an arts centre called Summerhall and there is a pub next door called The Royal Dick. Simple, really. The whole operation is done by hand and distillation takes place on two stills called Gert and Emily, after the founders' maternal grandmothers. This version has a red wax seal, and the navy strength one has a busby. Don't ask. The gin itself is very good indeed and has picked up a number of awards.

Plymouth Gin

PRODUCER: Pernod Ricard

ABV: 41.2%

REGION AND COUNTRY OF ORIGIN: Plymouth, England

WEBSITE: www.plymouthgin.com

BOTANICALS: Juniper berries, coriander seed, orange peel, lemon peel, green cardamom, angelica root, orris root

Few cities or towns can claim a stronger relationship with gin's history than Plymouth. Gin production in the Southwest English port can be traced back to the 1790s, and the British Navy bought huge volumes of Plymouth Gin in the following century. The distillery has links to America's founding fathers, with the Pilgrim Fathers spending their last night on the property before joining the *Mayflower* and sailing into the future. The gin is now owned by Pernod Ricard, but it has maintained its simple but impressive traditional gin recipe. This is a versatile and outstanding gin that shouts 'craft' despite its multinational ownership.

Pollination gin

PRODUCER: Dyfi Distillery

ABV: 45%

REGION AND COUNTRY OF ORIGIN: Machynlleth, Wales

WEBSITE: www.dyfidistillery.com

BOTANICALS: Not disclosed, but including juniper berries, coriander, unwaxed lemon peel, bog myrtle, Scots pine tips, wild flowers, aromatic leaves, and fruits

Dyfi Distillery was formed in 2016 by brothers Danny and Pete Cameron. Pete, a hill farmer and beekeeper, moved to the Dyfi Valley in Wales thirty-five years ago. Danny worked within the wine industry and, between them, they came up with the idea of making gin that represented the valley, which is recognized by UNESCO as a World Biosphere Reserve, and which has flora and fauna unique to it. This gin contains nine classical botanicals and twenty native and wild foraged botanicals, which are chosen for their taste, with consideration made as to the ideal time of the year to forage them and from what part of the valley. The gin is made in two one-hundred-litre stills specially made for them in Colorado.

Portobello Road No 171

PRODUCER: Thames Distillers for Jake Burger

ABV: 42%

REGION AND COUNTRY OF ORIGIN: London, England

WEBSITE: www.portobelloroadgin.com

BOTANICALS: Juniper berries, angelica root, orris root, lemon peel, orange peel, liquorice root, cassia bark, nutmeg

This is the gin created by bar supremo Jake Burger in association with Thames Distillers. The name refers to the location of The Ginstitute, London's second smallest museum and a place where a small still is used for making gin with visitors to the building. It's a cool part of London, and this is a cool gin. Burger and partners Ged Feltham and Paul Lane spent nine months settling on nine botanicals to make a gin that is winning an increasingly sizeable following within the bar trade. It's a beautiful, simple, but clever mix of refreshing and clean juniper and citrus, with dancing and playful spices. A great cocktail gin.

Sacred

PRODUCER: Sacred Spirits Company

ABV: 40%

REGION AND COUNTRY OF ORIGIN: London, England

WEBSITE: www.sacredspiritscompany.com

BOTANICALS: Twelve botanicals, including juniper berries, cardamom, nutmeg, hougary frankincense

Ian Hart and partner Hilary Whitney are living the dream. They have a small gin distillery in their North London home and are making a range of exciting gins, vodkas, and vermouths for an ever-growing audience. They have more than one hundred botanicals stored away, including Somerset wormwood and macerated plum and cherry stones. This particular gin was chosen by patrons of a local pub, who tried each of Sacred's gin recipes before settling on this one at the twenty-third attempt. The name comes from the inclusion of frankincense in the recipe, and Sacred makes a range of other gins, each one highlighting a different botanical. Particularly interesting are a grapefruit-led gin, an aged negroni mix, and a Christmas pudding gin.

Sipsmith

PRODUCER: Sipsmith

ABV: 41.6%

REGION AND COUNTRY OF ORIGIN: London, England

WEBSITE: www.sipsmith.com

BOTANICALS: Juniper berries, coriander seeds, angelica root, liquorice root, orris root, almond, cassia bark, cinnamon, orange peel, lemon peel

It could be argued that this is where the British gin revolution started. Sam Galsworthy and Fairfax Hall, two entrepreneurs with considerable drinks industry experience, successfully applied to make gin in West London and recruited drinks expert Jared Brown as a consultant, to set about creating a bespoke London gin. That was in 2009 and now Sipsmith has moved to bigger premises, enjoys masses of respect, and has successfully managed to balance far larger distribution and a reputation as a true craft distiller. This is partially to do with the fact that the distillers release some superb seasonal and limited-edition spirits-based drinks.

St George Terroir Gin

PRODUCER: St George Distillery

ABV: 45%

REGION AND COUNTRY OF ORIGIN: California, USA

WEBSITE: www.stgeorgespirits.com

BOTANICALS: Juniper berries, angelica root, bay laurel, cardamom, cinnamon, coastal sage, coriander, Douglas fir, fennel seed, lemon peel, orris root, Seville orange peel

California's St George Spirits was founded in 1982 by master distiller Jörg Rupf. Over more than three decades, at the vanguard of the American craft spirits movement, the distillery has grown into a diversified operation with a portfolio that includes single malt whiskey, agricole rum, absinthe, and several gins, vodkas, brandies, and liqueurs. It is now owned and operated by master distiller Lance Winters and head distiller Dave Smith. This gin is called Terroir because it is an attempt to re-create the aromas, atmosphere, and beauty of the forest behind the distillery. The botanicals have been chosen to capture woodsy fir tree and pine. It's earthy, rustic, distinctive, and unique. Clever work, guys!

ST. GEORGE

ARTISAN DISTILLERS SINCE 1982

TERROIR

GIN

A uniquely Californian gin
with a sense of place and poetry,
inspired by the wild beauty
of the Golden State

45

45% ALC. BY VOL.

Strathearn Heather Rose Gin

PRODUCER: Strathearn Distillery

ABV: 40%

REGION AND COUNTRY OF ORIGIN: Perth, Scotland

WEBSITE: www.strathearndistillery.com

BOTANICALS: Juniper berries, coriander seeds, orange peel, lemon peel, liquorice root, rose petals, purple heather flowers

Strathearn was set up as Scotland's first microdistillery for single malt whisky production. It is certainly one of the smallest, with all its equipment fitting into one room and its whisky spirit capacity about 30,000 litres. A small team of four started producing gin in 2013 and, although the first whisky has now been released, gin production has continued. This gin has heather and rose among its ingredients, as its name suggests, and looks more like whisky until tonic is added, when it takes on a distinctive pink hue. The distillers describe it as a celebration gin and suggest serving it in a flute, topped up with tonic.

SW4

PRODUCER: Thames Distillers

ABV: 40%

REGION AND COUNTRY OF ORIGIN: London, England

WEBSITE: www.sw4gin.com

BOTANICALS: Juniper berries, coriander seeds, angelica, cinnamon, orange peel, orris powder, nutmeg, savory, cassia, almond, lemon peel, liquorice

This gin is named after the postcode of the distillery in Clapham, South West London. A conventional but stylish gin, it is the brainchild of a former marketing director of British drinks distributor Maxxium. It is positioned at the top end of the premium gin market. With an ingredients list that reads like a 'who's who' of traditional botanicals and a big emphasis on juniper, this is clearly aimed at re-creating an older late 19th-century style of gin, as distinct from the current crop of new releases aimed at the cocktail sector and gin and tonic market. A weightier, 47% ABV version, called, er, SW4 47, is also available. Both are highly enjoyable.

Tanqueray No TEN

PRODUCER: Diageo

ABV: 47.3%

REGION AND COUNTRY OF ORIGIN: Cameronbridge, Scotland

WEBSITE: www.tanqueray.com

BOTANICALS: Juniper berries, angelica root, coriander seeds, liquorice root, camomile flowers, fresh orange peel, fresh grapefruit peel, fresh lime

Tanqueray is one of the great names of gin. The standard London Dry Gin was originally made to a simple recipe by Charles Tanqueray. The brand is now owned by international drinks giant Diageo at its huge Cameronbridge distillery, but the original still is still used there. Tanqueray No TEN – named after the still it is distilled in. Although this gin is made to the same basic recipe as the standard version, it uses fresh citrus fruits, which are added into the gin to give it flavours that the producers say make it perfect to make a martini. A third gin, Tanqueray Rangpur, is also on the market, and that includes a strong lime theme.

Tappers Darkside Gin

PRODUCER: Tappers

ABV: 39.6%

REGION AND COUNTRY OF ORIGIN: West Kirby, England

WEBSITE: www.tappersgin.com

BOTANICALS: Eight botanicals, including juniper berries, red clover, chickweed, sea beet, spicy black cardamom seeds

The name of this comes from the affectionate term given to the Wirral Peninsula in England's Northwest by day trippers from Liverpool who venture over to the 'dark side' of the River Mersey to visit quaint seaside towns and villages. 'Darkside reflects local, good-natured rivalry and doffs a hat to the region's maritime history,' say the distillers.

There are eight botanicals in Darkside Gin including a unique range of coastal ingredients such as red clover (adding a honey-like sweetness), chickweed (for herbal undertones), and freshly foraged sea beet. We also use peppery and spicy black cardamom seeds, rather than the usual green cardamom, to add a little kick up front on the mouth. It is an unusual gin with some highly attractive maritime notes. It is made in small batches and individually bottled, labelled, and wax-sealed by hand.

TAPPERS

DarkSide

SMALL BATCH ARTISAN GIN

An invaluable hand-crafted preparation offering
positive relief for the mind and body

39.6%
vol

50cl
℮

Tarquin's

PRODUCER: Southwestern Distillery

ABV: 42%

REGION AND COUNTRY OF ORIGIN: Wadebridge, Cornwall

WEBSITE: www.southwesterndistillery.com

BOTANICALS: Juniper berries, coriander seeds, sweet orange zest, lemon zest, grapefruit zest, angelica root, orris root, green cardamom seeds, bitter almond, cinnamon, liquorice root, Devon violets

The Southwestern Distillery lies on the North Cornwall coast in the south of England. It's a region that has its own Celtic language, a distinct culture, and a strong claim to national independence. Unsurprisingly, it has developed a culinary tradition independent of England, with nods to its Celtic cousins in Brittany to the south. So here, in addition to gin, the founder and head distiller makes pastis. Gin is made in small batches on a small flame-fired copper pot still called Tamara, named after the goddess of the River Tamar, which separates Cornwall from the English county of Devon.

Telser Liechtenstein Dry Gin

PRODUCER: Marcel Telser

ABV: 47%

REGION AND COUNTRY OF ORIGIN: Liechtenstein

WEBSITE: www.telserdistillery.com/Gin/Liechtenstein-Dry-Gin

BOTANICALS: Juniper berries, angelica root, camomile, cinnamon, coriander, elderflower, ginger, lavender, lemon peel, orange peel

Marcel Telser comes from a family with 140 years' history of spirits production and he's obsessive about quality distilling, working closely with The Alpine Spirits Producers, who educate any potential distillers in Germany, Austria, and Switzerland. There are scores of distilleries in the region, most of which are producing fruit liqueurs but are increasingly experimenting with single malt whisky production. He makes a distinctive and unique single malt whisky in Liechtenstein, and he has succeeded here in making a gin that is as fresh and clean as the Alpine region the distillery lies close to. This is an enjoyable but quite floral gin.

TELSER
FÜRSTENTUM LIECHTENSTEIN
HANDCRAFTED SINCE 1880

LIECHTENSTEIN
DRY GIN

Small Batch
Distilled London Dry Gin

Refined with finest
alpine herbs and blossoms

DISTILLED & BOTTLED BY
DISTILLERY TELSER
TRIESEN, LIECHTENSTEIN
brennerei-telser.com

50cl   47% Vol.

The Botanist

PRODUCER: Bruichladdich

ABV: 46%

REGION AND COUNTRY OF ORIGIN: Islay, Scotland

WEBSITE: www.thebotanist.com

BOTANICALS: Juniper berries, apple mint, camomile, creeping thistle, downy birch, elder, gorse, hawthorn, heather, lady's bedstraw, lemon balm, meadowsweet, mugwort, red clover, sweet cicely, spearmint, tansy, bog myrtle, water mint, white clover, wild thyme, wood sage

Some gins have six botanicals, some ten. But The Botanist has a whopping twenty-two, and is the drink equivalent of a lengthy nature trek round the island of Islay, off Scotland's west coast. Islay is known as the whisky island, and it's the home of some of the big smoky whiskies, made with grain dried over peat fires. Indeed, this gin is made by whisky distillery Bruichladdich. The botanicals have been collected from the island and the gin itself is distilled very slowly on the distillery's Lomond still, which is affectionately known as 'Ugly Betty'. Distilling takes about seventeen hours and the resulting gin is floral, complex, and beautifully balanced.

The London No 1

PRODUCER: Thames Distillers

ABV: 47%

REGION AND COUNTRY OF ORIGIN: London, England

WEBSITE: www.thelondon1.com

BOTANICALS: Juniper berries, cinnamon sticks, orange peel, angelica root, almond, iris root, savory, bergamot, liquorice, lemon peel, coriander, cassia

In many ways, The London No 1 epitomizes the relationship between London, gin, and the worldwide trade in botanicals. The brand itself is owned by Gonzalez Byass but it is made by Thames Distillers in Clapham, South West. The twelve botanicals reflect the huge international trade in herbs and spices based around London in the past, and they come together to create a classic London-style gin. These days London No 1, stylishly packaged, maintains a strong international connection, and its website follows events in the world's leading style bars such as Unico in Shanghai and the Bombay Club and Martini Bar.

Two Birds Gin

PRODUCER: Mark Gamble

ABV: 40%

REGION AND COUNTRY OF ORIGIN: Market Harborough, England

WEBSITE: www.twobirdsspirits.co.uk/ourspirits

BOTANICALS: Juniper berries, orris root, angelica root, citrus peel, coriander

Made in my home town of Market Harborough, Leicestershire, by Mark Gamble, this is a stylish, beautifully produced, and deceptively simple gin, made with just five botanicals. The gin is made in one-hundred-bottle batches in a small twenty-five-litre copper still. This is the core gin and it has won a number of awards, proving that you don't need to add the kitchen sink to make great gin. The distillery makes a range of gin products including an Old Tom gin, a special cocktail gin, and a wood-aged sipping gin, as well as a range of innovative vodkas and an absinthe. If you fancy being a distiller for the day, then this is the place to contact, as in 2017 it started offering all-day workshops.

Van Wees Three Corner Dry Gin

PRODUCER: A. van Wees de Ooievaar

ABV: 42%

REGION AND COUNTRY OF ORIGIN: Amsterdam, Netherlands

BOTANICALS: Juniper berries, lemon peel

Van Wees is the last traditional and authentic distillery in Amsterdam and is best known for its genevers, liqueurs, and bitters, but it makes a number of gins too, including this one. The family history goes back to the 1780s and, until fifty years ago, the distillery delivered its products by cask to a range of local bars and restaurants. The distillery's reputation is built on its traditional practices and its expertise with the use of fruit, plants, seeds, and roots. In one genever the distillery uses distilled rose petals. This, though, is as simple as it gets, with only lemon peel added to the juniper berry distillate. This is a clean and fresh gin, with both ingredients making their presence known.

Vidda Tørr Gin

PRODUCER: Oslo Händverksdestilleri (OHD)

ABV: 43%

REGION AND COUNTRY OF ORIGIN: Oslo, Norway

WEBSITE: viddagin.com/product/vidda/

BOTANICALS: Juniper berries, heather, yarrow, camomile flower, bilberry, angelica root, meadowsweet

This is an important distillery for Norway because it restored independence to the distilling sector after a gap of nearly ninety years. Vidda means 'mountain plateau' and, although this is an interpretation of a traditional British dry gin, it is infused with Nordic botanicals. It is made with herbs and spices that accentuate the flavours found on the mountain plains. It is a floral-forward gin, with meadowsweet and heather flower balanced by intense juniper notes. The distillers say that the taste has been designed to reflect the natural beauty of Norway and the clean mountain forests. Short growing seasons in Norway mean that the herbs and spices develop intense flavours, say the distillers.

Warner Edwards Harrington Dry Gin

PRODUCER: Warner Edwards

ABV: 44%

REGION AND COUNTRY OF ORIGIN: Harrington, England

WEBSITE: www.warneredwards.com/gins

BOTANICALS: Juniper berries, angelica root, black pepper, cardamom, coriander seeds, cinnamon, elderflower, lavender, orange peel

Warner Edwards is the business partnership of Tom Warner and Sion Edwards, who set out to create a distinctive product that was farm-made, hand-finished, and steeped in provenance. This is made in a 200-year-old barn in the picturesque village of Harrington in Northamptonshire. The distillery produces a range of small-batch, award-winning gins using the farm's natural spring water, grain spirit, and home-grown ingredients. Each batch is small, and every single bottle is hand-crafted by the team, from the filling to the wax seal and label finishing. The distillers put the high quality of their gins – and they are excellent – down to their purpose-built copper still, which they call Curiosity. A second still called

Satisfaction has been installed, and the team is using it to experiment with botanicals from its very own botanicals garden.

Whitley Neill

PRODUCER: Whitley Neill

ABV: 42%

REGION AND COUNTRY OF ORIGIN: Birmingham, England

WEBSITE: www.whitleyneill.com

BOTANICALS: Juniper berries, angelica root, baobab fruit, Cape gooseberry, cassia bark, lemon peel, orange peel, orris root

The Whitley in the name is a reference to brewing and distilling company Greenall Whitley, and Johnny Neill, the man behind this gin, is a member of that family. This gin is described as 'the heart of Africa distilled in England'. It is the product of Johnny's discovery of some old Greenall Whitley bottles at his grandmother's house, and his passion for Africa. His gran taught him about botanicals and made him, he says, an alchemist. His wife, who is African, told him exotic tales and inspired the choice of the Cape gooseberry and the fruit of the baobab tree, known as the tree of life. This gin is distilled in Constance, England's oldest still, at Langley.

Whittaker's Navy Strength Gin

PRODUCER: Harrogate Distillery

ABV: 57%

REGION AND COUNTRY OF ORIGIN: Harrogate, England

WEBSITE: www.whittakersgin.com

BOTANICALS: Juniper berries, angelica root, coriander seed, hawthorn berries, bilberries, bog myrtle, garden thyme, lemon citrus

Whittaker's of Harrogate in North Yorkshire is husband-and-wife team Toby and Jane Whittaker, and their distillery is as artisanal as it gets, having pretty much been built by friends and family. The couple had got interested in operating a craft brewery from their farm but, while studying brewing and distilling at Heriot-Watt University in Edinburgh, Toby set his heart on distilling instead. The ingredients are local and are macerated for twenty-four hours. Natural water from the farm is used and the gin is distilled in two copper stills. Both stills are named Jezebel after their daughters Jessica and Isabella, and both are one-hundred-litre stills imported from Bourbon, Kentucky. The standard version of this gin has an ABV of 42%.

Wight Mermaids Gin

PRODUCER: Isle of Wight Distillery

ABV: 42%

REGION AND COUNTRY OF ORIGIN: Isle of Wight

WEBSITE: www.isleofwightdistillery.com

BOTANICALS: Juniper berries, rock samphire, Boadicea hops, English coriander seeds, fresh lemon zest, angelica root, liquorice root, orris root, elderflower, grains of paradise

This is the original gin from the Isle of Wight Distillery, which is the island's first ever distillery. It makes a special vodka and has a gin that is linked to the famous *HMS Victory*, just across the water on England's mainland. The distillery also now does a moonshine which it calls Apple Pie. This gin includes rock samphire, which is hand-picked from the island's chalk cliffs, Boadicea hops grown on the island at the Ventnor Botanic Garden, and English coriander seeds. All the ingredients are steeped for twenty-four hours before distillation and are allowed to rest for seven days, once distilled, before bottling.

Wild Island Botanic Gin

PRODUCER: Colonsay Beverages

ABV: 43.7%

REGION AND COUNTRY OF ORIGIN: Colonsay, Scotland

WEBSITE: wildislandgin.com

BOTANICALS: Juniper berries, coriander seeds, lemon peel, orange peel, liquorice, cinnamon bark, angelica root, orris root, cassia bark, nutmeg, lemon balm, wild water mint, meadowsweet, sea buckthorn, heather flowers, bog myrtle

Colonsay is a remote rocky Scottish island some two and a quarter hours from the mainland, and it is, indeed, a wild island, a mix of long sandy beaches, rocky outreaches, and stunning natural beauty. About one hundred people live here, and it's known for its fresh oysters and honey from its native black bee. There is also a general store and a brewery. And it's from the brewery that this gin comes. Take a look at the botanicals and it's clear how strong an influence Colonsay's landscape has had on this gin. The gin is produced in small batches on a copper still and only 750 bottles are released at a time. This is a gin of exceptional quality.

Williams Elegant Crisp Gin

PRODUCER: The Chase Distillery

ABV: 48%

REGION AND COUNTRY OF ORIGIN: Herefordshire, England

WEBSITE: williamschase.co.uk/collections/gin

BOTANICALS: Juniper berries, angelica root, angelica seeds, Bramley apple, elderflower, hops, lemon peel, liquorice root, orange peel, orris root

This is a genuinely different proposition as a gin, with apple spirit used as its base and the inclusion of hops among the botanicals. You wouldn't expect anything different from the Chase stable. William Chase was a potato farmer, who decided to make crisps in his kitchen with a batch of potatoes that had been rejected by a supermarket. This was the start of his Tyrrells Crisps business, which brought crafted crisps to the marketplace and broke the big-brands monopoly, and which he would go on to sell for £40 million. Then he turned his attentions to an innovative potato vodka. The distillery also makes liqueurs now, and its range includes a grapefruit gin and a Seville orange gin. One of the pioneers, Chase can be relied on for exceptional quality.

CHASE

Williams
Elegant
48

GIN

Elegant
— 48 —
GIN

GROWN, DISTILLED
AND BOTTLED BY HAND
ON OUR HOME FARM IN
HEREFORDSHIRE, ENGLAND

48% Vol 70cl℮

Worship Street Whistling Shop Cream Gin

PRODUCER: Worship Street Whistling Shop

ABV: 43.8%

REGION AND COUNTRY OF ORIGIN: London, England

WEBSITE: www.whistlingshop.com

BOTANICALS: Not disclosed, but including cream!

The Worship Street Whistling Shop is a cool bar in the East End of London, close to Shoreditch, which is modelled on the old Victorian gin palaces. The team behind it are among the country's best mixologists and they have been championing gin and gin cocktails for way longer than it's been trendy to do so. Gin mixed with cream was highly popular at one time, and this version is a collaboration between the bar and the online retailer, Master of Malt. This version of it is made by cold distilling and using cream as a botanical. It has a different mouth feel to most spirits. The bar uses it as a core ingredient in its signature cocktail, the Black Cat Martini. As stylish as it gets.

Index

6 O'clock 16–17
60 Squared 18–19

A
acacia flowers 154
Adnams Copper House 20–21
aged gins 14
allspice 92, 154
almond 28, 34, 40–44, 94, 176, 182, 188, 194
    bitter 34, 188
angelica 10, 18, 22, 30, 36–40, 82, 86, 94–8, 106, 114, 120, 148, 154, 166, 182
angelica root 15, 28, 34, 42–6, 52, 56, 62, 66–8, 78–80, 84, 88–90, 102, 112, 116, 126, 140, 152, 160, 164, 168, 172, 176, 184, 188, 190, 194–6, 200–10
angelica seed 28, 50, 212
anise/aniseed 24, 164, 166
Anno Kent Dry Gin 22–3
Anty Gin 50
apple 52, 212
apple mint 192
Aviation American Gin 24–5

B
bamboo leaves 134
baobab fruit 204
base spirits **9, 10, 46,** 134
basil 30, 50, 104
bay laurel 178
bay leaf, Cotswold 62
Beefeater 26, 28–9
bergamot 194
Berkeley Square 30–1
bilberry 120, 200, 206
bitter root 92
Black Shuck 32–3

blackberry 120, 154
blackcurrant leaf 50
Blackwater No.5 Gin 34–5
Blackwoods Vintage Dry Gin 36–7
blaeberry 136
blending 11
Bloom 38–9
blueberry 58
Boë 40–1
bog myrtle 52, 72, 170, 192, 206, 210
Bombay Dry Gin 42–3, 44
Bombay Sapphire 10, 42, 44–5, 116
borage 102
botanicals 9–15
    see also specific botanicals
Botantist, The 192–3
Broker's Gin 46–7

C
Cadenhead's Classic 48–9
Cambridge Dry Gin 50–1
camomile 18, 22, 38, 116, 154, 184, 190–2, 200
Cannonball 88
Caorunn 52–3
Cape gooseberry 204
caraway seed 78, 116
cardamom 20, 34, 40, 78, 80, 96, 100, 104, 106, 126, 166, 168, 174, 178, 202
cardamom seed 15, 62, 186, 188
carob 96
casks 14, 120
cassia 68, 74, 98, 118, 148, 182, 194
cassia bark 22, 40–46, 52, 66, 84, 100, 114, 120, 126, 152, 164, 172, 176–8, 204, 210
cassia quills 34, 48, 160
cassis 96
Chase Distillery, The 212

chickweed 186
cinnamon 34–6, 46–8, 54, 68, 76, 96, 114, 160, 176, 178, 182, 188–90, 194, 202, 210
Citadelle 54–5
citrus 76, 104
citrus peel 36, 88, 122, 126, 196
City of London Gin 56–7
cloves 68, 106, 152–4, 166
cocktails 7, 24, 28, 36, 172, 214
cocoa 82
coconut 124
Cold River 58–9
Conncullin Gin 60–1
copper berry chambers 52
copper stills 78, 92, 96, 100, 126, 202, 206
coriander 10, 18–19, 22–4, 32–48, 56, 62, 66, 70, 78, 100–106, 112–18, 140, 148, 154, 160–62, 166, 170, 178, 190, 194–6
coriander seed 15, 20, 28, 30, 52, 68, 74, 80, 84–98, 120, 126, 144, 152, 168, 176, 180–4, 188, 202, 206–10
Cotswolds Dry Gin 62–3
crab apple 120
cream 214
cubeb berry 18, 22, 30, 38–40, 44, 84, 96, 100, 116, 162
cucumber 116, 128, 148
cumin 68, 152, 162

D

Da Mhile Seaweed Organic Gin 64–5
Daffy's Gin 66–7
damson gin 16
dandelion leaf 52
Darkside Gin 186–7
Darnley's View Spiced Gin 68–9
Death's Door 70–1
defining gin 9
Dingle Gin 72–3
distillation 9, 12
Dodd's Kew Organic Gin 74–5

Dorothy Parker 76–7
Douglas Fir 178
downy birch 192
Drumshanbo Gunpowder Gin 78–9
Dutch Courage Dry Gin 80–1

E

East India Company London Dry Gin 82–3
East London Liquor Premium Gin Batch No 1 84–5
Eden Mill Pink Love Gin 86–7
Edinburgh Gin 88–9
elder 192
elderberry 76, 86, 154
elderflower 16, 60, 116, 190, 202, 208, 212
Eletaria cardamomum 24
ethyl alcohol 9
eucalyptus 74
extraction 11

F

fennel 70, 166
fennel seed 178
Fifty Pounds Gin 90–1
Filliers Dry Gin Tangerine 92–3
Finsbury Platinum 94–5
flavoured gins 15, 112
Flemish OriGIN 96–7
Fords 98–9
frankincense, hougary 174
fuchsia 72

G

gardener's hope 154
génépi 54
genevers 12–13, 80, 96, 198
gentian root 96
Gilpin's 102–3
Gin Act 1736 90
Gin Mare 104–5
gin palaces 6, 13
gin and tonic 6, 11, 72, 74

Ginerosity 106–7
ginger 40, 68, 92–6, 100, 124, 134, 154, 190
Ginstitute, The 172
Glendalough Wild Botanical Gin 108–9
goji berries 86
Gordon's 11
Gordon's Export 110–11
gorse 192
grains of paradise 12, 44, 68, 90, 96, 122, 154, 208
grapefruit 62, 78
pink 84, 124
grapefruit peel 15, 28, 56, 74, 98, 162, 164, 184, 188
Greenall's 30, 38, 112, 138, 162
Greenall's Original 112–13
G'Vine Floraison 100–1

H
hawthorn 72, 154, 192
hawthorn berry 60, 206
Hayman's Royal Dock 114–15
heather 52, 72, 88, 106, 180, 192, 200, 210
Hendrick's 116–17
Hernö 118–19
Hibernation 120–21
hibiscus 20, 76, 86
Hill Gin 26–7
hinoki 134
history of gin 5–8
HMS Victory Naval Strength 122–3
honey 26
honey pomelo 154
honeysuckle 38
hops 18, 22, 96, 208, 212
Hoxton 124–5

I
immersion 10
Inverroche Classic 126–7
iris 94, 124, 194

J
Japanese Gin 50, 128–9
jasmine 98, 154
Jensen's Bermondsey Gin 130–1
juniper 5, 7, 9–10, 13, 15–16, 18, 20–22, 30, 34, 76–8, 82, 160
juniper berry 15, 24–8, 32, 36–62, 66–74, 80, 84–106, 112–28, 136–40, 144, 148–54, 158, 162–76, 178–212
Junipero Gin 132–3

K
kaffir lime leaves 18, 22, 30
kelp 136
Kent Dry Gin (Anno) 22–3
Ki No Bi Gin 134–5
kinome 134
Kirsty's Gin 136–7

L
lady's bedstraw 192
Langton's No 1 138–9
lavender 18, 22–4, 30–32, 62, 74, 92, 96, 190, 202
Lebanese mint 66
lemon 10, 18, 22, 34, 40, 66, 78, 106, 112, 116, 120, 134, 166, 206
lemon balm 192, 210
lemon myrtle 106
lemon peel 28, 42–8, 52, 56, 74, 80, 90, 94–8, 102, 114, 118, 138, 144, 148, 158–60, 164, 168–72, 176, 178–82, 188–90, 194, 198, 204, 208–12
lemon verbena 50
lemongrass 34, 74
Liechtenstein 190
lime 62, 106, 166, 184
oriental 78
lime peel 74, 94, 100, 102, 148
lingonberry 118, 120
liquorice 18, 22, 36, 40, 48, 56, 74, 82, 96, 100, 114, 120, 138, 160, 182, 194, 210
orange 154

liquorice root 28, 34, 42–6, 80, 90, 148, 158, 172, 176, 180, 184, 188, 208, 212
Listoke 1777 140–1
Liverpool Gin 142–3
London Dry Gin 6, 13, 42, 56, 82, 110, 114, 130, 184
London gin 9
London Hill 144–5
London No 1 194–5

M

Makar 146–7
making gin 9–11
malt 92
mandarin 92
marsh marigold 36
marshmallow man 154
marshmallow root 86
Martin Miller's Westbourne Strength 148–9
Mascaró Gin 9 150–1
meadowsweet 36, 78, 118, 164, 192, 200, 210
milk thistle 88
mixologists 7, 11
Mombasa Club 152–3
Monkey 47 Schwarzwald Dry Gin 154–5
mugwort 192
musketeer 154
myrtle pepper 34

N

neutral grain spirit 9
No 3 gin 156–7
Nolet's 158–9
Norwegian gins 200–1
Nouaison 100
nutmeg 36, 46–8, 54, 68, 74, 96–100, 114, 148, 154, 160, 172–4, 182, 210

O

oak 14, 26, 138
Old Raj 160, 160–1

Old Tom 11, 13–14, 118, 130, 146, 196
olive, Arbequina 104
Opihr Oriental Spiced 162–3
orange 40, 106
bitter 18, 22, 34, 102
orange blossom 92
orange peel 10, 16, 46, 52, 56, 66, 80, 90, 94–6, 114–16, 138, 158, 162, 168, 172, 176, 180–4, 190, 194, 202–4, 210–12
bitter 32, 98, 148
fresh 164
Seville 28, 48, 160, 178
sweet 15, 20–24, 144, 188
orris 48, 120, 134, 160
orris powder 98, 182
orris root 20, 22, 28, 34, 40–46, 66, 74, 78–82, 88, 96, 114–16, 148, 158, 164, 168, 172, 176–180, 188, 196, 204–12
oude (jonge) 12–13
Oxley 164–5

P

peach, white 158
pepper
black 62, 118, 202
Tellicherry black 162
Pernod Ricard 28, 168
Perry's Tot 76
Pickering's 106, 166–7
Plymouth Gin 168–9
Pollination 170–1
pomelo 38
Portobello Road No 171 172–3

Q

quinine 6

R

raspberry 158
raspberry leaf 86
red clover 186, 192
red shiso leaves 134
rhubarb root 86

rice spirit base 134
rock samphire 208
rose 50, 86, 116, 180
Turkish 158
rosehip 18, 22, 154
rosemary 50, 74, 96, 104
rowan berry 52, 72
Royal Dock 114–15

S

Sacred 174–5
saffron 160
sage 30, 102, 154, 178, 192
St George Terroir Gin 178–9
samphire, Kentish 18, 22
sansho pepper 128, 134
santolina 74
sarsaparilla 24
savory 182, 194
scarlet monarda 154
Scots pine tips 170
sea beet 186
sea buckthorn 32, 210
sea pink 36
seaweed 64, 136
sesame seed 128
shiso leaf 128
Sikkim 15
Sipsmith 176–7
sloe gin 16, 112
spearmint 192
spruce shoots 154
star anise 78, 96
steeping 10
stills 16, 22, 166, 170, 192, 204
column 6
copper 78, 92, 96, 100, 126, 202, 206
pot 10, 46, 74, 78, 92, 96, 126
Strathearn Heather Rose Gin 180–1
SW4 182–3
sweet cicely 192

T

Tanqueray No TEN 184–5
tansy 192

Tappers Darkside Gin 186–7
Tarquin's 188–9
tarragon 124
tea
Darjeeling 84
green 28, 134
gunpowder 78
Japanese sencha 28
Telser Liechtenstein Dry Gin 190–1
thistle 96, 136, 192
thyme 104, 192, 206
Tom Cat 26
tonics 11
Two Birds Gin 196–7

V

Van Wees Three Corner Dry Gin 198–9
vanilla 80, 118, 164
vapour extraction 10
vervain 154
Vidda Tørr Gin 200–1
vine flowers 100
violet 50, 188

W

Warner Edwards Harrington Dry Gin
  202–3
water mint 192, 210
wheat 46, 70
white clover 192
Whitley Neill 204–5
Whittaker's Navy Strength Gin 206–7
Wight Mermaids Gin 208–9
wild flowers 170
Wild Island Botanic Gin 210–11
Williams Elegant Crisp Gin 212–13
wood sage 192
Worship Street Whistling Shop Cream
  gin 214–15

Y

yarrow 96, 116, 200
yeast 12
yuzu 128, 134

Picture Credits

The publishers would like to thank the following for their assistance with images:

Adnams plc, Blackwater Distillery, Bramley and Gage Ltd, Broker's Gin Ltd, Bruichladdich Distillery, Caledonia Spirits, Caorunn Gin, Chase Distillery, Colonsay Beverages, Daffy's, De Moor Distillery, Death's Door Spirits, Dyfi Distillery, Emporia Brands Ltd, Filliers Distillery, Ralf Roletschek / fahrradmonteur.de, G'Vine Gin, Glendalough Distillery, Greenall's, Harrogate Distillery Ltd, Hernö Gin, Inverroche Distillery, Isle of Wight Distillery, Jensen's Gin, Kyoto Distillery, Langton's Gin Ltd, Montserrat Mascaró, Norfolk Sloe Company, Park Place Drinks Ltd, Pernod Ricard, Portobello Road Gin, Shannon Sturgis, Sipsmith, St George Distillery, Summerhall Distillery, Tappers Gin, Telser Distillery Ltd, Thames Distillers, The Cotswolds Distilling Company Ltd, The East London Liquor Company, The Glasgow Distillery Company, The London Distillery, The Reformed Spirits Company Ltd, Two Birds Spirits, Warner Edwards, Wemyss Malts, William Grant & Sons, Zuidam Distillers BV

Andy Gibson, Angus McComiskey, Granger Historical Picture Archive, Keith Homan, Kevin George, Peter Horree, ZUMA Press Inc / ALL Alamy Stock Photo

Chris Fleming, Dominic Lockyer, Eric Gravengaard , Ewan Munro, Social Enterprise UK, Tim Parker / ALL CC BY 2.0

Grossmatthias1234, Travellingbajan / CC BY-SA 4.0

aiaikawa, Alliance, beta7, bonchan, Cgissemann, ChiccoDodiFC, gueriero093, Hans Geel, John A Cameron, JurateBuiviene, kostrez, Kurbatova Vera, lokvi, mama_mia, Margaret Clavell, Marten_House, Melpomene, Mint and Lemon, monticello, natashamam, picturepartners, Quanthem, Riekelt Hakvoort, urbanbuzz, walshphotos, Yolanta / ALL Shutterstock.com

Collins

LITTLE BOOKS

These beautifully presented Little Books make excellent pocket-sized guides, packed with hints and tips.

Bananagrams Secrets
978-0-00-825046-1
£6.99

Bridge Secrets
978-0-00-825047-8
£6.99

101 ways to win at Scrabble
978-0-00-758914-2
£6.99

Whisky
978-0-00-825108-6
£6.99

Scottish Castles
978-0-00-825111-6
£6.99

Scottish Dance
978-0-00-821056-4
£6.99

Scottish History
978-0-00-825110-9
£6.99

Clans and Tartans
978-0-00-825109-3
£6.99

Available to buy from all good booksellers and online.
All titles are also available as ebooks.
www.collins.co.uk

 @collins_ref    facebook.com/collinsref